FRIEN

I dedicate this book to my remarkable husband,

my most loyal and beloved friend.

FRIENDING

Creating Meaningful, Lasting Adult Friendships
© Gina Handley Schmitt, MA, LMHC, 2019
This Edition © Microcosm Publishing 2019
First published November 12, 2019

ISBN 978-1-62106-750-4
This is Microcosm #309
Edited by Elly Blue
Cover by Cecilia Granata
Interior Illustrations by Trista Vercher
Book design by Joe Biel

For a catalog, write or visit:
Microcosm Publishing
2752 N Williams Ave.
Portland, OR 97227
www.microcosmpublishing.com

Names, identifying information, and circumstances have been changed in the interest of privacy.

If you bought this on Amazon, I'm so sorry because you could have gotten it cheaper and supported a small, independent publisher at www.Microcosm.Pub

To join the ranks of high-class stores that feature Microcosm titles, talk to your rep: In the U.S. **Como** (Atlantic), **Fujii** (Midwest), **Book Travelers West** (Pacific), **Turnaround** in Europe, **Manda/UTP** in Canada, **New South** in Australia, and **GPS** in Asia, India, Africa, and South America.

Global labor conditions are bad, and our roots in industrial Cleveland in the 70s and 80s made us appreciate the need to treat workers right. Therefore, our books are MADE IN THE USA and printed on post-consumer paper.

Library of Congress Cataloging-in-Publication data:

Names: Schmitt, Gina Handley, author.
Title: Friending : creating meaningful, lasting adult friendships / Gina
 Handley Schmitt, MA, LMHC.
Description: Portland, OR : Microcosm Publishing, [2019]
Identifiers: LCCN 2019020127| ISBN 9781621067504 (pbk.) | ISBN 9781621062554
 (e-book)
Subjects: LCSH: Friendship. | Trust. | Interpersonal relations.
Classification: LCC BF575.F66 S366 2019 | DDC 158.2/5--dc23
LC record available at https://lccn.loc.gov/2019020127

MICROCOSM·PUBLISHING

Microcosm Publishing is Portland's most diversified publishing house and distributor with a focus on the colorful, authentic, and empowering. Our books and zines have put your power in your hands since 1996, equipping readers to make positive changes in their lives and in the world around them. Microcosm emphasizes skill-building, showing hidden histories, and fostering creativity through challenging conventional publishing wisdom with books and bookettes about DIY skills, food, bicycling, gender, self-care, and social justice. What was once a distro and record label was started by Joe Biel in his bedroom and has become among the oldest independent publishing houses in Portland, OR. We are a politically moderate, centrist publisher in a world that has inched to the right for the past 80 years.

CONTENTS

INTRODUCTION

Ten years ago, one of my therapy clients invited me to go to a movie. There was a new film in the theaters that she was convinced we would both enjoy (and I was convinced that she was right), but I had to carefully explain to her that while I was flattered by her invitation, due to our professional relationship, I was not actually ethically permitted to accompany her to a movie, however much we might both have enjoyed the film. She cried.

As we processed the reason for her emotional response, she confided that I was her only "friend." She shared that she did not know how to make adult friendships. She also shared that any efforts she had made to connect with other peers in the previous few years had ended in her feeling rejected, leaving her feeling even more alone, and fearing she was destined to be so permanently.

This sweet client was to be the first of many who would sit on my therapy couch and confide in me their struggles to make meaningful, enduring friendship connections. Some of these clients had lost their connections over the years due to their changing life circumstances. Others had never developed these meaningful connections in the first place. But either way, one thing was the same: all of them were desperately wanting healthy, long-term friends—as I have come to believe most of us do.

The more this situation played itself out in my counseling practice, the more I realized that our society was experiencing a "crisis" of sorts. In fact, my research since then has revealed that 25% of adults report having *zero* trusted confidants. That is 1 in 4 people without a single person to share the most intimate parts of their lives with.[1] *One in four.* I realized that this lack of meaningful, enduring friendship connections in our society seemed to be driving more and more people to my therapy couch in an attempt to fill this void. But for those who were lonely but could not afford therapy, I wondered what replacements they had chosen. These hard realities motivated me to think more seriously about how this had happened, what societal factors may have contributed, and what I might know that could help people struggling to make and keep adult friends.

My quest to understand this friendship crisis led me to think more about the relevant shifts in our society over the last few decades, as we have almost completely changed the way we interact with our friends. Only 20 years ago, we didn't have smart phones and lightning fast internet connections. If we wanted to connect, we would have to issue a face-to-face invitation for an in-person hangout. Or, at least, we'd have to pick up a landline, dial a telephone number, and have a voice-to-voice conversation. Today, if we want to connect, we can email, text, message on Facebook, tweet, send a Snapchat—the list goes on. We have so many more means for communicating, but many of these means seem more conducive to creating a multitude of shallow connections and few, if any, deep, intimate connections. Social media provides us with the opportunity for

---

1 Matthew Lieberman, *Social: Why Our Brains are Wired to Connect* (New York: Crown Publishing, 2013).

quantity but not necessarily quality. We each have hundreds of "friends" on Facebook, but 42.6 million American adults report suffering chronic loneliness.[2] I don't think the correlation between the rise in technology dependence and the rise in adult loneliness is a mere coincidence.

I use and enjoy many online platforms for connecting with friends, and I wholeheartedly believe that technology can aid in facilitating and enhancing our friendships. Research indicates that the moderate use of technology in our friendships is not intrinsically harmful to the relationships, and that regular "reciprocated social media posting" can actually yield significant relationship rewards. That said, the research is also clear that technology can be problematic when relied upon as the main sustenance for our friendships.[3] So, the challenge, then, is to ensure that we have balance in our relationships, and that we don't find ourselves with innumerous online "friends," while simultaneously being chronically lonely.

My ongoing research on loneliness suggests that it has more far-reaching effects than we may realize. Loneliness can increase a person's risk of early death by more than 26%—more than a long-term smoking habit or consistent exposure to air pollution. Alternatively, close friends can decrease our tension, stress, and depression, while increasing our bodies' defenses and our overall life satisfaction.[4] So, while our society might be tempted to treat friendship as a mere luxury, research reminds us that it is actually a necessity for both our physical

2 G. Oscar Anderson, "Loneliness Among Older Adults: A National Survey of Adults 45+," *AARP Research*, September, 2010.
3 Dunbar RIM, "The Anatomy of Friendship," *Trends in Cognitive Sciences*, January 2018.
4 Julianna Holt-Lunstad, Timothy B. Smith, and J. Bradley Layton, "Social Relationships and Mortality Risk: A Meta-analytic Review," *PLoS Med* 7, no. 7 (July 2010), https://doi.org/10.1371/journal.pmed.1000316.

and emotional health. In fact, a lead researcher for a major study out of Harvard concluded from his team's findings that "the only thing that really matters in life are our relationships to other people."[5]

In addition to considering societal shifts over time and accompanying research, I have also spent a significant amount of time reflecting on my own personal friendship-making journey. In addition to being a therapist and relationship expert, I am also a forty-something woman who has herself been lost in the process of creating meaningful, enduring friendships many times. I have moved over a dozen times throughout my life, and, with that, have had to start or restart many friendships over the years. This has been no easy task, and I have experienced the loneliness that often accompanies being the "new kid" more times than I care to remember. However, these experiences have also offered me the opportunity to practice meeting new people and creating new friendships. Through all of these experiences, I have come to wholeheartedly believe that making and keeping good friends is essential to our universal need for connection and sense of belonging.

A few years ago, I was invited to speak at a local women's conference. As I was preparing for my Saturday session, it seemed that all of my previous thoughts and ideas on friendship, my research, my client's stories, and all of my own friendship struggles over the years culminated in this opportunity to share with a broader audience. This motivated me to create the friendship-making and -keeping criteria that I have used as the foundation for this book. These are the same criteria that I ultimately hope will assist anyone who is looking for meaningful connections with friends, but who has found themselves lost or disillusioned in that process.

Since speaking at that first conference and further cementing my friendship making criteria, I have been increasingly motivated to share my research, insight, and experience (including both my personal and professional stories) with as many people as I can, in as many different environments as possible. As I have been on this sharing mission, I have continued to hear things like, "I really wish I had had these tools sooner." So finally, here I am completing this book on friendship, this labor of love that has been years in the creating, hoping that anyone longing for meaningful, enduring friendships will find their way to these pages. Whether you are someone who finds themselves desiring more from their current friendships, someone who is trying to create friendships in a new season of life, or someone who, like my sweet client, feels alone and destined to be so permanently, I hope you will leave feeling encouraged and equipped to dive into deeper friendships.

As we officially begin our journey together, I want to formally introduce you to the five relationship skills that I believe, when used together, will provide you with a firm foundation for healthy, long-term connectedness. First, we will learn how to be *available*. This skill serves as the foundation for any friendship. Second, we will learn how to be *authentic*. This skill is essential to fostering deep connections with our friends, as it allows us to commit to mutual honesty and vulnerability. Third, we will learn how to be *affirming*. This skill ensures that our friendships ultimately become safe and encouraging spaces. Fourth, we will learn to be *assertive*. This skill ensures that we are getting what we need from our friendships, while also serving to protect and preserve them. Finally, we will learn to be *accepting*. This skill will not only help us recognize the potential in new friendships, but it will also assist us in offering our existing friends more grace, within the context of our potential differences.

I am hopeful that the skills outlined above will help each reader create pathways for improving their interpersonal skills and will ensure that they are contributing to meaningful, enduring friendships. So, with this ultimate goal in mind, I officially invite you to join me for what I hope will be five chapters of encouragement, empowerment, and practical tools for creating or maintaining the healthy adult connections we all need and deserve.

BEING AVAILABLE

We have all had times in our lives when access to friends came more easily—when we were more available to spend time with our friends or to meet new friends. For some of us, this was our childhood—afternoons spent riding our bikes around the neighborhood or playing soccer in the street in front of our apartment complex. For others, it was adolescence—participating in the school play or traveling with the high school basketball team to away games. Or maybe for some this came in young adulthood—working at a local restaurant, attending college, or traveling abroad.

For me, it was my college years. This was, by far, the season in my life most conducive to creating friendships. I had easy access to countless peers every day at morning chapels, cafeteria lunches, and late-afternoon psychology classes. There were just *so many* opportunities for connection. If I was ever lonely, I needed only walk down my dorm hallway and knock on a few doors, and I would find someone up for any number of shenanigans (or at least a late-night Taco Bell run). Those were the days, and I didn't even know not to take them for granted.

Even in my twenties and early thirties, it seemed there were still quite a lot of opportunities for getting together with friends. Perhaps this was because I had more energy and fewer demands on my free time. Or perhaps this was because I had not yet become so dependent on technology as a means for connecting with my people. Whatever the reason (or reasons), though, maintaining deep connections with friends has gotten more and more difficult as the years have passed.

Now, it seems my friends and I have to plan a get-together *months* in advance. Even then, at least one or two people will need to cancel at the last minute due to an unexpected work demand, the flu, or just plain exhaustion from all the stress of adulting. Being with my favorite people has become an increasing challenge, and it can grow tiring to put forth the effort, especially when the time together can be fraught with interruptions.

That said, I am incredibly grateful to have a faithful group of close friends, that I lovingly refer to as my T-Town crew (because most of them live in Tacoma, WA). We have all made a collective commitment over the last decade to celebrating a number of annual traditions together. While we do have to work *really* hard sometimes to find mutually agreeable dates and times, we are committed to that time together and make it a priority to be available. When my life gets overwhelming and I feel like I might drown in the pure mayhem of it all, I can look at my calendar and count down the days until I can be with these cherished friends again. It is such a relief to be assured that my favorite people will all be gathered in one place together at least three or four times each year.

We will all wear green and eat corned beef and soda bread for St. Patrick's Day. We will hunt for and carve pumpkins for our beloved Pumpkin Patch Day (rain or shine). And, we will eat spaghetti and watch our favorite holiday movie, *Elf*, at our silly and enjoyable Elf Night celebration—every year. Sometimes we also get the added treat of a Cinco de Mayo fiesta, a Fourth of July cookout, or, most recently, a 40th birthday party—crazy costume edition. Even though getting together is not as easy as it used to be, these times spent with my closest friends are some of the highlights of my adult life, and I can't imagine not having them to look forward to.

And so, the challenge for this chapter will be to encourage and equip us all in making time for friendship. I hope we can create opportunities to spend quality time with our established friends, and to make ourselves more available for cultivating new friendships. Regardless of the season of life we are in, I wholeheartedly believe that we can all be more available in our relationships . . . physically, emotionally, mentally, and, if pertinent, spiritually.

The Art of the Long Lunch: Being Available For Our Friends *Physically*

While every friendship or friendship group might negotiate their togetherness in a different way, it probably goes without saying that we cannot create meaningful connections without spending quality time together. We need this togetherness to foster familiarity, comfort, and intimacy. If we are going to create or maintain deep friendship bonds, then, at the very least, we are going to have to commit to showing up for coffee dates and weekend bike rides and communal celebrations. We are going to have to make the necessary time for *being with* each other.

In order to make these get-togethers happen, we will have to initiate invitations. Whether that takes the form of an old school, face-to-face invite, a phone call, a text message, or a Facebook post, we need to offer invitations to the people we want to spend time with. If we are attempting to start a new friendship, or missing someone local, we can propose a walk-and-talk in the coming week. If we are missing someone less local, we can start planning a visit, or at least schedule a Skype or FaceTime session, so we can see each other's sweet faces. Whatever our circumstances, we need to make a commitment to initiating togetherness, because we need to get those friend dates on our calendars before they completely fill up with all of the adulting responsibilities.

If you're not quite sure how to initiate a hangout invitation with a new potential friend, it could be as simple as:

> *Hey, I would love to get to know you more, as you seem like a really cool person. I notice you ride a bike to work. Would you like to go for a ride with me sometime? And maybe grab a coffee after?*

If you're not quite sure how to initiate a hangout invitation with a friend you haven't seen in a while, you could say:

> *Hey, there. We have not had the chance to connect in a while, and I miss catching up with you. What does your schedule look like this month? Could we get lunch together sometime when we're both available?*

Listen, these invitations don't have to be elaborate or painstaking. It's not important that the invitation is perfectly worded or executed. The important thing is that they happen, providing us an opportunity to create or maintain our friendship connections.

My friend Mon-Lin and I have become the *queens* of the long lunch. After working together for a couple of years at a group practice in the Seattle area, we developed quite a bond. We laughed easily and often when we were together, so when we went our separate ways professionally, we committed to staying in touch. Even now, years later, every couple of months one of us will reach out to the other with a long lunch invitation. Once together, we will inevitably eat copious amounts of delicious food, while reminiscing about the terrors of our final days at the group practice and the ups and downs of our lives in the here and now. We are both busy people, and it would be easy to let the relationship fall by the wayside, but we decided—and continue to decide—that the effort is worth it. And we both leave those long sharing fests feeling encouraged and refreshed (and very, *very* full).

When we are able to get these kinds of meet-ups with our friends firmly in our calendars, it is important that both people in the relationship look forward to and enjoy this time together. Any relationship will struggle if there is an imbalance in the commitment to this quality time. If one person is always enthusiastic about the togetherness and the other is disengaged or distracted, it usually does not bode well for ensuring that both people in the friendship feel equally valued. Without this, trust and intimacy are virtually impossible to maintain. And without trust and intimacy, the friendship will almost certainly dissipate. So, I challenge us all to find and spend time with friends who are as excited about eating delicious lunches together as we are.

Each friendship will establish its own unique "rules" about how often this face-to-face time is required to maintain a meaningful connection. For some friends, this might be weekly. For some, it's annually. For some, it's somewhere in between. As long as both people are being honest about their needs for quality time and are content with the dynamic, the friendship can remain healthy. That said, I also find that the more time we spend with our friends, the healthier we tend to be. In fact, research suggests that those of us with an intimate network of friends tend to have less stress, stronger immune defenses, and a longer life expectancy. Friends also ward off depression and help us in overcoming illnesses, while also increasing our overall happiness.[6] So, I highly recommend that we make time with friends a priority and create opportunities for togetherness as often as possible.

There may be times in a friendship when we receive a hangout invitation and our schedules don't cooperate. This is a pretty normal scenario for most adult friendships. Most of us have had to decline a hangout with someone we really enjoy simply because we have a mandatory work meeting, or a previously scheduled volunteer commitment, or a date night with our partner that we were *finally* able to pull-off. So, if you are on the receiving end of an invitation that you must decline, welcome to the club. But also, the ball is now in your court to find another time that might work for both of you, and to extend the next invitation.

There may also be times in a long-term friendship where one person is less available than the other due to more challenging life circumstances rather than a lack of enthusiasm

6 Julianna Holt-Lunstad, "Social Relationships and Mortality Risk," July 27, 2010. https://doi.org/10.1371/journal.pmed.1000316

about the friendship. This could be due to a personal physical illness, the illness of a loved one, a recent break-up, or a bout of depression. Whatever the reason for this change, it is important that we are patient during these times, while also committing to talking openly about what has changed and what the expectations are for preserving the relationship during this specific timeframe. Or, if a friend has a chronic illness, we may need to discuss how we can maintain a connection when face-to-face time might be off the table for the foreseeable future. Whatever the circumstances, though, honest communication is key whenever a relationship dynamic changes.

If you realize that you need to have one of these conversations, I would recommend starting with something like:

"I have noticed that you've been understandably preoccupied with all that you have going on right now, and we have not been able to find a lot of time for hanging out. Do you want to try to make a monthly date? Or can we agree that our lives are hectic right now, and that's okay? I don't want to lose our connection in the midst of difficult life circumstances, as our relationship is really important to me."

Sometimes acknowledging the change and communicating an openness to an ongoing dialogue is the biggest and best step towards ensuring that a friendship remains healthy.

This last year, I have had some prohibitive medical issues that have made me less available for face-to-face hangouts with friends. We have had to change some of the ways we connect in order to compensate for these disruptions, and I have been so grateful for the grace I have received. My friends have done a great job of making me feel included (and missed), and I have learned a lot about how I want to treat friends going through hardships. So, while showing up for your friends physically is vital to maintaining healthy connections, it is also important to develop skills for offering grace to friends who are simply unable to be physically present for a period of time.

If you have a friend who is less available, consider how you might regularly communicate your unconditional love and appreciation for them. Could you invite them to regular phone call dates? Send text messages to check-in? Throw a thoughtful card in the mail? Or send them a gift basket of their favorite goodies? Whatever you do to communicate your gracious acceptance of and empathy for their circumstances will almost certainly be appreciated, probably more than you realize. And, hopefully, this care might be reciprocated one day if you are ever in a similar situation.

One final note on being physically available for friends: As our society continues its trend toward online and smartphone connectedness, we will have to talk with our friends about how this is changing our relationship dynamics, and whether we are comfortable with the changes we are experiencing. Do we feel that our friendship can survive on regular Facebook engagement and occasional text messages? Or, are we craving more face-to-face time with our people? Do we need to create a better plan for being together more often? Or are we content with our current arrangement? Again, healthy, honest conversations are the key to ensuring that we are all getting the time we need with each other. If you are not currently having these conversations in your friendships, but are realizing through the reading of this chapter that you need to, I would encourage you to initiate a dialogue . . . sooner rather than later.

FRIENDING EXERCISES:

1. Is there a specific friend that you could reach out to with a hangout invitation this week? Jot down that person's name below, along with some thoughts about the invitation, and then plan a time to contact them tomorrow.

2. Are you getting your needs for face-to-face time met in your current friendships? If no, clarify your unmet needs below, make a plan for initiating a conversation with your friend(s), and then work toward a mutually agreeable resolution.

3. Have you found yourself allowing social media to drive your friendships lately? If yes, use the space below to process why and to think more about the quality of these interactions and whether they are meeting your needs for deep connection. If no, how might you pursue a better balance?

Distractions Be Gone: Being Available for our Friends MENTALLY

Have you ever taken a moment to look around a restaurant or coffee shop and noticed the sheer number of people sitting in the presence of other people, while . . . staring directly at their phones? These people appearing to prefer the company of an electronic device to the company of the human being that is sitting *right in front of them*? Have you ever *been* the person? I must admit that I have certainly been an offender—more than once. Most of us have. But I don't like it. Whether it's intentional or not—and I'm assuming most of the time it's not—the message we send when we do this is that we do not value the person in front of us as much as we value whatever else we are doing on our phones. Ouch.

While showing up physically for friends is important for connectedness, showing up mentally is just as important. Showing up physically without showing-up mentally is counterproductive if our goal is genuine connection, because spending time with someone who is not mentally present feels . . . lonely. We have all been with a friend when they were distracted, and we can always tell when they are not really present—not hearing us. It can be a pretty hurtful experience. But in a society that is often moving at 100 miles per hour, it is certainly not uncommon to be either the offended or offender in this situation.

Working as a therapist means that I have to be especially conscious of this issue. In order to be effective at my job, I have to be mentally present all day long, as clients share their stories and struggles. As you can imagine, when I leave my office at the end of the day, I often find myself mentally fatigued. It can be difficult to offer my personal relationships any more mental or emotional energy when I've used so much of it throughout my work day. In order to ensure that my most important relationships are not neglected, then, I have to be incredibly purposeful about how I schedule time with the people in my life. I have to be mindful of what I can realistically offer, not commit beyond that, and try to avoid professional distractions from interfering with the time I do commit to my personal life. This awareness is something we could all benefit from in our relationships, regardless of our chosen professional fields.

Because we know that distractions are so readily available, it is important to decide ahead of time to limit them as much as possible when spending time with friends. In fact, I have some friends who insist on putting away all cell phones when we're together, realizing that there is nothing happening on social media that cannot wait an hour to be seen or "liked," and probably nothing happening at home that our roommate, partner, or babysitter can't manage for a little while. If for some reason our circumstances *do* require us to be available on our cell phone, for instance due to an on-call work situation or an ill child, let's be upfront with our friends ahead of time. When we find the time to get together face-to-face with our people— which seems to be increasingly rare—we all deserve to have each other's undivided attention.

As part of this ongoing challenge to be mentally available for our friends, I would also encourage us to focus on being increasingly mindful and intentional in our interactions. Friendships grow and thrive when we can be open, receptive, respectful, and compassionate. But they can be damaged when we are closed, critical, disrespectful, or dismissive of each other. Part of meeting this goal for being available for our friends mentally is ensuring that our contributions in this area are healthy and purposeful.

Different friendships might require different things from us, because every friendship dynamic is unique. Being available for our friends mentally means paying attention to what we (and our friends) need from the relationship. Some of us might need more cheerleading, while others might need more practical help fixing up our first home. Some might need weekly walk-and-talks, while others might need thoughtful cards in the mail. And still others might simply need more hugs. If these relationship needs sound familiar, it's because they are similar to the principles proposed by *The Five Love Languages*.[7] While initially intended for romantic relationships, a commitment

---

7 Chapman, Gary, *The 5 Love Languages: The Secret to Love that Lasts*, Chicago: Northfield Publishing, 2015.

to understanding our friend's "love languages"—the types of actions that make them feel valued—can be an important part of ensuring that we all feel fulfilled and connected longterm.

If you are unsure how to ask for your needs to be met in a friendship, you could simply start with:

"Hey, I was wondering if I could ask a friendship favor of you. I really love catching up and chatting about our favorite Netflix shows, but I'd also really appreciate it if you could throw more <insert your love language need here> my way, as I am realizing I really need that to feel supported and connected to you."

By being honest and specific in this way, hopefully we can find some mutually agreeable plan to ensure that both people are getting what they need from the relationship.

Finally, if we know that our current life circumstances are not conducive to being fully mentally engaged with our friends—for whatever reason—it's okay to admit that before we get together. It is okay to send a simple text and communicate that we are not on top of our game, so we can decide together what would be in the best interest of both friends (and the relationship) as we approach the next step. Sometimes we might decide that we can get together anyway, and enjoy the time regardless. Or, we might decide to reschedule for another time. Either way, it's worth noting that we will all need to reschedule a get together at some time, and that is normal and perfectly fine, as long as conversations are honest and time together is still a priority.

FRIENDING EXERCISES:

1. Is there something tangible you could do to limit distractions while you are spending time with friends? If yes, jot down some thoughts below and consider implementing that strategy at your next friend date.

2. When attempting to show up mentally for your friends, do you find that you are consistently able to do so with openness and honesty? If no, what changes would need to happen for you to be able to be more available in this way?

3. Are there things that you need mentally from your close friends that you are not getting at this time? If yes, make a list below.

Coffee and Catharsis: Being Available for our Friends *Emotionally*

In order to have meaningful, enduring friendships, we need our people to show up physically, mentally, and *emotionally*. This means that we need friends who are capable of sharing their honest emotions and offering space and care for ours. We need our people to be able to talk about their lowest lows, as well as their highest highs, and we need them to be able to sit with us in ours.

I have a couple of girlfriends who are introverted. Like, *very* introverted. They don't share deep things in our group text messages, and they aren't the first ones to spill their guts when we all get together for an overdue share fest. So, I absolutely love the moment when, about an hour or so into our time together, one of them finally starts sharing from the heart. I know that's when we've reached the "emotional sweet spot" in the evening—when everyone at that table is feeling safe and able to be vulnerable. It feels like sacred friendship ground every single time.

I've come to believe that emotional safety is essential for meaningful, enduring friendships. This kind of emotional connectedness is what makes friendship so valuable, so sweet, and so necessary. It is a significant part of why I am writing this book. I really want this emotional intimacy for all of us, and I believe it is possible for us to have if we will make the necessary commitment to being emotionally available.

I have found that when this emotional component is missing in a friendship—when everyone is not feeling emotionally safe and not showing-up authentically—it is difficult to feel completely invested. Many times a deficit in this area will lead to a rather shallow dynamic, or one person carrying all of the burden for emotional connectedness—resulting in that person having "sharer's remorse," as they realize they are being vulnerable . . . *alone.*

So, if we are to nurture emotionally safe and healthy relationships with one another, we will need to be able to talk about this expectation of vulnerability. Both people in the friendship will need to share honestly about what they need and want. They will need to feel comfortable sharing their stories, and both people will need to feel capable of providing care for the other. If one or both people don't feel comfortable sharing in this way, then a meaningful, enduring friendship may not be feasible.

If you are not sure how to broach a discussion of this nature, or if the mere thought of such a discussion makes you cringe, then I am happy to report that I have some ideas for you. Start by simply acknowledging the issue:

"For some reason, I am feeling unable to be vulnerable in our friendship. I am not sure if I am having unrealistic expectations, or if there is some barrier keeping us from going deeper in our relationship. I would love to discuss it further, as I would really like to have a more connected friendship."

If your friend says, "Oh, thank God. Me, too. I wasn't sure how to bring it up, but I am so glad you did. Let's figure it out," then you have won the friendship conversation lottery, and you can make your way from there.

If you are met with something like, "I like our friendship the way it is," or "I don't really have a desire for that brand of vulnerability in our friendship," then you will have a decision to make. You can accept the terms of a more surface level friendship, or you can consider if it might be time for a friend break-up.

If you are not sure how to negotiate a healthy friend "break-up," you might start by saying:

"Thank you for your honesty. If I'm being honest, I need more from my friendships right now. I respect your decision, but I also realize that it's not consistent with my own needs at this time, so I am going to take a step back from the relationship for now."

Listen, I know break-ups are rough, so I don't want to be too cavalier about this. But, I have also come to believe that being honest with ourselves and our friends about the need for a break is better than continuing in a relationship that is not mutually satisfying, which will almost inevitably lead to mounting frustration and bitterness. So, if you find that a friend is not willing or able to contribute to the relationship in a way that is conducive to the meaningful, enduring friendship dynamic that you need, then it might be time to admit that to yourself and to your friend. Do it kindly. Do it carefully. But do it. And consider reallocating that relationship energy into a friendship that is capable of meeting your needs for connectedness.

I also want to take a moment to acknowledge that some of us might identify more with the friend on the receiving end of this break-up scenario. We might have internalized messages about making ourselves emotionally available that go something like: "I don't think I could ever be fully vulnerable in a relationship. I don't think I could share my deepest thoughts and emotions with another person. I don't trust people to provide the type of care you are describing. I have just been hurt too many times." If this is you, I want you to know that I acknowledge your struggle. You are not alone. I have heard this from dozens of clients and friends over the years, and if we were face-to-face right now, I would normalize your feelings and offer you genuine compassion. And then, I would tell you . . . I think it's time. It's time to deal with whatever pain you have experienced in your past relationships, time to heal, and time to stop allowing yourself to be stuck. You deserve meaningful, enduring friendships. And, with healing and help, I believe you can find them.

If you don't know where to start the process of finding and creating emotionally healthy friendships—like so many of us struggle to do at different points in our lives—I would encourage you to think about the people in your life who you genuinely like. Look for the people you see being emotionally healthy and open, the people who treat others with respect, the people who seem to have space at their table. You don't need much else to start the friending process. You just need an emotionally healthy, kind, available person. If you can think of anyone in your life who meets that criteria—and I'm sure most of us can—then I would encourage you to issue a hangout invitation this coming week.

Hopefully, a meaningful, enduring friendship will blossom from this initial hangout at the pub after work, authentic conversation over tea, or shared volunteer outing. It only takes *one* of these shared experiences for the seed of friendship to be planted, and then the emotional connection can grow from there, as you each commit to consistently showing up emotionally. You don't have to be best friends after your first hangout. Let the friendship evolve organically and try to simply enjoy the process.

While I am genuinely hopeful that your friendship attempts will all beautifully and perfectly blossom in the way described above, I do want to offer a little counsel about setting realistic emotional expectations for our friendships. There are many different types of friendships that can occupy many different spaces in our lives. And while this book is most concerned with finding and keeping deep, connected friendships, I also want to spend some time talking about other kinds of friendships and their potential value.

I had a delightful client many years ago who consistently struggled with a sense that she was oversharing in her relationships. Zoe was quite open and incredibly loquacious, so we both understood how this might be happening. Together, we committed to working on better discerning the "who" and "how" of sharing her deep, emotional thoughts and feelings. In this endeavor, we used a "Friendship Circle" exercise to help us clarify which relationships in her life were most appropriate for intimate sharing.

This "Friendship Circle" included a center circle, where we placed Zoe herself. In the circle immediately surrounding her, we placed the people who she *loved* and who *loved* her, namely her intimate friends. This included her friends from childhood, a couple of close friends from her gaming community, and a few friends from her small group at church. These were people she could share the most intimate parts of her story with, and who she usually had contact with on a daily or weekly basis.

We then placed the people Zoe *liked* and who *liked* her in the next circle. This included a couple of close colleagues, a friend from her volunteer work, and a few more people from her

gaming community. These were the friends she could count on for consistent support and with whom she regularly shared her good and bad news. These were friends who she usually had contact with on a weekly or bi-monthly basis.

Finally, we placed the friends (or acquaintances) who didn't really know Zoe well enough to commit to liking or loving her in the final circle. This included a few additional colleagues and acquaintances from her different recreational activities. These were friends who she enjoyed spending time with, but whom she only had meaningful interactions with a couple of times a year. These might be people who made her Christmas newsletter list, but not people who were actually invited to the intimate Christmas gathering at her small condo.

With her Friendship Circle complete, Zoe had increased awareness about the relationships that would be most appropriate for deep, emotional sharing, and which relationships were not quite ready. Having these more realistic emotional expectations, Zoe was more able to enjoy all of her relationships for what they were and not ask of them more than they could offer. This left Zoe feeling better equipped and incredibly relieved.

Long before Friendship Circles were a thing, Aristotle suggested 3 similar types of friendships in his writings: Utility, Pleasure, and Virtue.[8] These types provide a good reminder that friendships can occupy different parts of our lives and fulfill different relational and emotional needs. While this book's main goal is helping us identify and nurture what Aristotle called "virtue" friendships, I also wholeheartedly believe that we can enjoy all three of the friendship types identified, and even see

8 Aristotle. *Nicomachean Ethics.* 350 BC.

our friendships grow from one type to another over time. So, let's explore each of them a little more.

Utilitarian Friendships: These friendships are born out of a shared responsibility or goal. These friends (or acquaintances) might be our colleagues from the office, our fellow volunteers at the local animal shelter, other parents at our children's schools, or moderators on a forum we help manage. While we may sincerely like these people, and will have certainly shared some meaningful experiences together, these may not always be the relationships most appropriate for the sharing of our deepest emotions, as that is not the understood goal of our partnership. Most often, our immediate goals are more related to things like completing the budget proposal for our meeting the next day, spearheading a puppy rehoming project, hosting a successful bake sale to pay for a needed school gym remodel, or ensuring forum contributions are appropriate. Certainly, time spent together can lead to opportunities for a growing connection, but at their core, utilitarian friendships do not have deep emotional connectedness as their main goal.

Pleasure Friendships: These friendships are more focused on shared recreation, fun, and pleasure. These friends (or acquaintances) might include teammates from our recreational soccer league, fellow book lovers from our monthly book club, people we spend every other Wednesday night with playing trivia at the local pub, or people in our online gaming guild. This will undoubtedly include people that we have shared some laughs with, and they are also people we really enjoy spending time with. But, again, these relationships, at least initially, might not be able to fulfill our needs for deep emotional connectedness, as we are spending most of our time together running around kicking a ball, discussing book plots, answering trivia questions in a loud bar environment, or defeating the last raid boss. These relationships could certainly grow over time, but at their core, these connections are predominantly focused on having fun together.

Virtue Friendships: These are the friendships in which we will have invested significant time fostering togetherness and vulnerability. These are our long-term friendships with the people who have shared some of our most important moments. The people who have weathered storms with us. The people we most love and trust. They are our peeps, our crew, our family of choice, and they have earned the right to our deepest and truest selves. Unlike the other two kinds of friendship, virtue friendships *do* have deep connectedness as their most important goal, and thus they are the most valuable relationships we can have.

Again, the ultimate goal of this book is to help you find and nurture those virtue friendships in your life. But, time spent working side-by-side toward a shared goal or time spent laughing and playing is never time wasted. We may even find that some of our closest friendships find their origins in these shared utilitarian or pleasure experiences.

My final challenge for this chapter is that we learn to identify relationships (and the surrounding circumstances of those relationships) that are appropriate for deep emotional sharing, and that we ensure that we are capable of this sharing when opportunities arise. I believe Aristotle has certainly provided us some help in that process, but I would also encourage us all to more fully hone the art of awareness and acceptance, by paying attention to cues from the peers we have the opportunity to interact with on a regular basis. Simple cues like eye contact, engaged body language, and mutual curiosity and vulnerability can all help us in distinguishing which friendships could be appropriate for a deeper investment. My ultimate hope is that we all be capable of being open and emotionally vulnerable (when we feel safe to do so), while also being capable of discerning relationships that are not appropriate or ready for deeper emotional intimacy.

FRIENDING EXERCISES:

1. Do you have any emotional barriers in your life that would stop you from being able to connect fully with friends?

2. How are you feeling about the level of vulnerability in your friendships? Is there enough openness? What are you contributing or not contributing to this dynamic? Take some time to process, and then list steps for making any necessary changes.

3. Fill in this Friendship Circle of your own

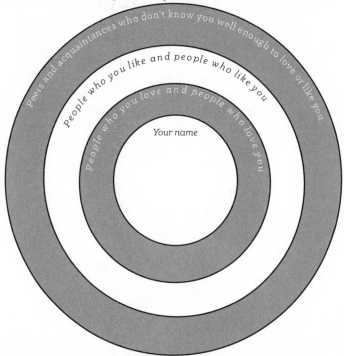

4. Where would most of your friends fit in Aristotle's friendship categories? Are you satisfied with those current dynamics? If no, clarify how you might go about making necessary changes, paying specific attention to the potential for transitioning friends to more relationally satisfying categories.

Sharing Our Spark: Being Available for our Friends *Spiritually*

Albert Schweitzer famously penned, "Often our own light goes out and is rekindled by some experience we go through with another person. Each of us has cause to think with deep gratitude of those who have lighted the flames within us."[9] Wow! What a powerful image and worthy friendship goal. It perfectly summarizes what it means to be available for our friends spiritually.

For some of us, our faith or spirituality is an important part of our lives, and thus becomes an important part of some of our friendships. We often look to our friends to help us in the

---

9 Albert Schweitzer, *The Light Within Us*. (New York: Philosophical Library), 1959.

exploration of our faith, as we attempt to further understand its role in our lives. Sometimes we invite friends to accompany us as we ask the hard questions about the relevancy and applicability of our faith. Other times we rely on friends to help us in healing from religious backgrounds that have left us hurt and resentful. During times of disillusionment and heartbreak, we look to our friends to bolster our faith as we face life's seemingly unfathomable tragedies and wonder about how faith fits into all of the messiness that is life.

I spent my high school years very involved in my church. After high school, I attended a Christian college. After Christian college, I attended a seminary for my graduate education. My first job after graduate school was at a faith-based foster and adoption agency. I spent most of my twenties and early thirties very involved in the faith community. However, these last few years I have found that faith has not come as easy. I have struggled with some difficult life circumstances, which, along with some increasing disillusionment with my faith experience, have left me feeling a bit disconnected from my faith. It has been disorienting at best and devastating at worst.

As I have been working through this difficult time, I have reached out to some of my good friends for wisdom and encouragement. I have been so heartened by their responses. Some of them have said things as simple as, "With you," and "Going through a similar season," and "I respect and honor your honesty and your struggle." I will never forget the potent words of a longtime, cherished friend, "I do not have all of the answers to your many questions, but I will certainly cry with you about how difficult and messy life can be." What a healing balm these responses were for my weary soul, as I so needed this offering of solidarity, understanding, and affirmation—without judgment. I have come to believe that this kind of unconditional love and support is what a faith community should be about. Heck, this is what friendship should be about.

While my personal frame of reference for spirituality has been predominantly Christian, I have had the opportunity to come alongside friends and clients from a variety of faiths. I have consistently found that meaningful, enduring friendships seem to be an important component of almost all belief systems. A few years ago I had the opportunity to work with a dear client who was making a transition from the Christian faith he inherited from his family, to Buddhism, which was more aligned with his adult faith needs. As he was navigating the transition, he was finding it difficult to make close friends within his new faith community. As we processed this concern in our sessions, we decided to do some research on the role of friendship in the Buddhist tradition to hopefully find some inspiration and motivation for this part of his journey. I was so heartened when my client shared the following story with me.

> In an ancient Buddhist story, the Buddha's faithful attendant, Ananda, asked about the importance of having wholesome companions. Ananda asked the Buddha whether having noble friends and companions wasn't half of the holy life. The Buddha replied: "Do not say so, Ananda. Noble friends and companions are the whole of the holy life."

I absolutely love this story and come back to it often, as it not only places such a high value on friendship, but also because it is such a great reminder that this desire and need for faithful companions is a pretty universal one. It also happened to be the exact encouragement my client needed to further pursue and create the friendships he desired in his new faith community. Yay!

While supporting and encouraging friends who share the same faith system as you is important, it is also important that we be available and supportive of our friends who might have a different religious practice than we do. Part of the challenge of being available for our friends spiritually is offering care and concern for the people in our lives who might think about faith differently than we do—or people who might not subscribe to a faith system at all. Loving and respecting our friends means making space for our spiritual differences, and continuing to listen to and understand each other through that process.

And so, my closing challenge is to use our faith to foster connection with the people in our lives, to manifest our spirituality in ways which support, encourage, and offer hope to our friends, and to use our sparks to help rekindle those of our friends in need.

FRIENDING EXERCISES:

1. Do you have a friend who is struggling with their faith and/or spirituality? Use the space below to brainstorm how you might go about offering them a listening, non-judgmental ear.

2. Do you need to give yourself permission to share some of your faith struggles with your friends? If yes, take some time to clarify below. Then, commit to a time this coming week to share more honestly with your people.

3. What would a healthy spirituality look like for you, and what might it contribute to your life and relationships?

BEING AUTHENTIC

Have you ever spent time in environments that put you at ease and made you feel more comfortable sharing your story? Perhaps a trusted therapist's office? Or a best friend's cozy couch? Have you also been in environments that made you shut down emotionally? Situations where you've thought, "Nope. Not safe. Not sharing. No way?" Though I have certainly experienced my fair share of "Nopes" throughout my life, I have been lucky to find more spaces that have been conducive to authenticity than not. One of my closest friends is especially gifted at fostering such spaces.

I remember when I first told Heidi that I had been abused as a young child. I had not shared that information with anyone in my friend circle, and before that night, I was not sure that I ever would. It was a painful secret that I kept tightly under wraps. So, sharing that secret with her one night on her couch was a big step—and a scary one.

But Heidi made my decision to be vulnerable less scary, because she listened to me, she believed me, and she offered me genuine empathy. I must have instinctively known that she would provide the safety that I needed, and that's why I chose her to confide in. You see, Heidi had also shared the most intimate details of her story with me, and thus I knew she would provide space and care for mine. She had paved the way for my authenticity with her unconditional love and care, and, most of all, with her own personal vulnerability.

Our twenty-year-long friendship has been full of deep and vulnerable conversations. Even before sharing about my abuse, I had confided in Heidi about my deep insecurities, toxic romantic entanglements, feelings of abandonment, and complex relationship with my family of origin. With each vulnerable disclosure, she consistently showed up with empathy, advice (when asked), and as an added bonus, an abundance of warm beverages and delicious treats.

It would be great if everyone could have a "Heidi" in their lives—someone who could provide space and care for their authentic stories, with all of their complexity and pain. So, that will be the challenge of this chapter. I want to encourage and equip us all in finding increasing ways to foster authenticity in our friendships, to be open and vulnerable in the sharing of our stories, and to provide safe and empathetic spaces for our friends to share their own stories.

Making Space for "The Real": Accepting Imperfection in Ourselves and Others

Being a psychotherapist means that people have a lot of misconceptions about how perfect my life must be—perfect marriage, perfect friendships, perfect family—and how perfect I must be in all of them. Many people think that because I am a psychotherapist, trained to help other people with their issues, that I have somehow completely perfected the art in my own personal life. And no one is sorrier than me to say—*it's just not true.*

I am a flawed, messy, and imperfect person, who is also a psychotherapist. The longer I do the job, though, the more I realize that it may be these very imperfections, and my awareness, acceptance, and commitment to working on them, that makes me good at helping other people with theirs. And this same principle holds true for our friendships. We can be the best friends to the people in our lives when we can make room for our flaws, and in doing so, give our friends permission to do the same.

More than ever before, we live in a society that seems to constantly scream, "Not good enough!" "Not pretty enough!" "Not enough!" Everywhere we look there is someone selling something to make us "better," always perpetuating the message that we need to be better than we are. Everything seeming to reinforce the belief that we are not enough—that we are lacking. And yet, after we buy, read, and do all of the things that will supposedly make us better, there is always some other elusive standard for "enough" that we haven't met—and we must start again. It can be maddening.

Now, I'm not saying that I don't love a good concealer as much as the next person. Or that trying a Paleo diet is wrong. Or that buying every Brene Brown book ever written is not a *very* worthwhile investment. What I am saying is that you don't have to spend your entire life chasing thing after thing, in hopes that it will finally make you enough. Because, regardless our imperfections, we *are* enough. I am enough. You are enough. No makeup or smaller jean size or "aha" moment is going to make us more "enough" than we already are.

There is a song that I absolutely love by Colbie Caillat called "Try." This song perfectly encapsulates our sometimes desperate pursuit for "enough." In fact, the lyrics provide a haunting list of all our crazy-making efforts—trying to change our physical appearance, trying to be "sexy," trying to have all of the newest and best fashions. Trying, and trying, and trying, and trying, until finally, Caillat issues us a potent challenge at the end of the song. She asks us to relinquish all of the exhausting striving and to just be. To look in the mirror and to finally accept ourselves. And, in doing so, to allow others to accept us as well.

But how do we get there? How do we stop the maddening cycle of perfectionism and accompanying self-doubt, so we can accept ourselves and our friends? Well, to begin with, I would prescribe realness and vulnerability and honesty about life and its imperfections . . . and also its gloriousness. In other words . . . *Authenticity*. If we are going to overcome perfectionism and embrace authenticity, we are going to have to practice replacing our old mental tapes with new tapes. We are going to have to *stop* every time perfectionism rears its ugly head in our lives, and we are going to have to speak truth to it. We are going to have to say:

> *"Listen, perfectionism, you are not a realistic, attainable goal for me. You have kept me insecure and emotionally isolated for too long, and I'm done. I choose* real*. I choose to be me."*

I know it is no easy thing to present your real self to the world, warts and all, but I believe it is a worthwhile challenge. And it can be accomplished if we will commit to consistently choosing authenticity over the facade of perfection. I believe this authenticity thing is the only thing that leads to the real, meaningful, connectedness thing.

In addition to our need to speak truth to the lies of perfectionism, we might also need to spend some time speaking truth to the lie that we are somehow unworthy of healthy friendships. When we have lived for too long with perfection as our guide, we get a skewed perspective, not only of ourselves, but also of other people. In our insecurity, we can start to believe that other people have actually attained this perfection that we find so elusive. We can start to see other people's lives through this lens, and with every misperception, we become more and more convinced of our unworthiness to be in relationships with other people who "have it all figured out." But I have good news. *No one* has it all figured out. No matter how beautiful their profile pictures might be, or how exciting their vacations might seem, we are all messy and imperfect. And we all need and deserve friends who are equally messy and imperfect in their own unique ways.

There will inevitably be things in our lives and in the lives of our friends that we will consistently struggle to embrace. Sometimes these struggles might even be legitimate. For instance, I used to have a real issue with being on time. I have been late to get-togethers more times than I care to admit. This was not something that I ever embraced about myself, and it was not something that I expected my friends to embrace about me, either. That is understandable, because it could be incredibly annoying—both for them and for me. The challenge of this section, then, is not that we fully embrace all of the annoying things about the people in our lives, but rather that we make space for them. That we make space for imperfection, for our collective flaws. Maybe we do communicate our frustration to our friends when it is appropriate, but we also learn to offer grace to each other, knowing that we have our own annoying things, too.

If living authentically is our goal, we must get comfortable making room for "the real." We must accept that "the real" is going to be messy at times. We must accept that "the real" is never going to be perfect. Because "the real" is real life. I have never met anyone who has found a way to live life completely immune from struggle, and bad hair days, and cellulite, and moodiness, and buyer's remorse, and workout aversion. Life is complicated, and that is okay. Or, at least, it just *is*. Accepting this for ourselves and our people is an important step in nurturing meaningful, enduring friendships.

FRIENDING EXERCISES:

1. What do you need to accept about your real life, so you can start living more freely and honestly with yourself and your people?

2. What do you need to accept about the real life struggles of your friends in order to offer them the grace and compassion they need and deserve?

3. What negative messages have you allowed to convince you that you are not worthy of healthy friendships? Use the space below to practice replacing those negative messages with positive truths about yourself.

When Life Is *Not* Good: Avoiding the Pretending Game

One of the biggest barriers to living authentically is our tendency to pretend. We live in a society where we are always "good." You know what I'm talking about. You are at the grocery store, and you happen to run into a friend and politely ask, "How are you doing?" And what do we all respond? "Good, thanks. How are you?" And the immediate response back? "Good." Because we are always "good." Right? Even if we had a fight with our partner that morning, burned our breakfast, missed our dentist appointment, and somehow managed to throw our keys in the dumpster—all before noon—we are still, somehow, "good." Because we feel like we always *have* to be "good."

But, we're not good all of the time, are we? Some days we're just exhausted. Overwhelmed. Disappointed. Depressed. Anxious. Afraid. Lonely. We are often so many things, and *none* of them are "good." And that's okay. I mean, I want us all to be good. But it's okay to not be good. It's okay to have a bad day. It's okay to have a terrible, horrible, no good, very bad day. And I wish we would all give ourselves and each other permission and space to have a day that's not so good.

There is a part in the movie *Alexander and the Terrible, Horrible, No Good, Very Bad Day* where the movie family gathers in a restaurant parking lot after a series of unfortunate events. The dad, played by Steve Carrell, who feels a responsibility to be positive for his family *all* the time, is having a major meltdown. He is letting out his frustration alone when his family unexpectedly joins him. He immediately feels ashamed when his wife and children witness him angrily kicking a trash can, and he quickly tries to positively reframe the horrible experiences of the day that have lead up to that moment. But the family affectionately gathers around him, and they each take turns kicking the trash can in solidarity, giving him the needed permission to acknowledge how awful the day has been and releasing him from the heavy responsibility of pretending that everything is fine, when it's not.

Every time I see that scene, I smile. Not because the family has gone through such an ordeal, but because it's a reminder of the fact that life is messy, and that it is okay to admit it. This scenario perfectly demonstrates how we sometimes just need our people to stand with us and join us in the kicking of life's trash cans.

I mean, what if instead of being "good" all of the time, we tried answering the polite inquiry of a friend with something more real? For example, "Thanks for asking. It's actually been a rough morning." Or, "Not the best morning I've ever had, but I'm hoping for a better afternoon." I'm not advocating with blindsiding an unsuspecting recipient with *all* of the messy details of our challenging morning, but we can find a balance. If we can be honest and still manage to hold onto healthy boundaries, this would be a step toward creating a society that makes room for real people, with real lives, and real bad days.

It is also important to think about how we might respond if a friend were to reply with a more authentic response to our inquiry about their day. If we were already anticipating their "good" and armed and ready with ours, how would we manage a change in our programmed scripts? If you're unsure, I might recommend something like, "Oh, no. I'm sorry it's been bumpy. Thank you for being real about it. I guess my day has had its fair share of bumps, too." Or, if you want to keep it really simple, you could simply offer your friend compassion by saying something like, "I'm sorry your day is off to a rough start." This simple change in our scripts could be another important step in supporting increased authenticity in our relationships.

One of the main goals of authenticity is the fostering of relationship dynamics where we can be honest with each other about our struggles, both big and small. We should be able to admit when we are worried or exhausted or need a little help. We should not feel like we have to put on an act for our people. We should be able to trust that they can handle the messiness of our lives, knowing that we can handle theirs. This giving and receiving of support and care during difficult times is foundational for meaningful, enduring friendships.

Sometimes trading in my "goods" for more authentic responses has been hard to do. I really love being happy and positive, and I really, *really* love making my friends laugh. It can be frustrating to find yourself in a season of life where the smiles and silliness and witty banter don't come as easily as they once did. But, it's also freeing to have your dearest friends allow space for you in the midst of your struggle, to accept you even when you can't provide a stand-up comedy routine at every get-together. We all need to be reminded about this brand of unconditional love and acceptance.

It is also worth mentioning here that during our most difficult seasons, we *may* need to call in some extra reinforcements. When life has us traversing the really rough terrain, and we are having a difficult time finding anything positive to contribute to our relationships, we might need to take a step back to assess how much we are asking of our friendships. It is important to consider whether our expectations are fair, and whether we might need more help than our friends can provide. If we are not quite sure, here are a few parameters: Are we calling our friends multiple times per day for weeks on end to process our complex emotions? Are we texting incessantly to vent about our circumstances? Are these calls and texts regularly interfering with our friend's work, family, and/or other commitments? Do we feel our friends starting to pull away, be less available for our calls, less responsive to our texts? If yes, maybe it is time to talk to our friends about it and invite them to help us find some supplemental support options.

If we're not sure how to initiate this kind of conversation with our friend, we can begin by acknowledging our awareness that we've been asking a lot of the friendship. We can ask our friend if they feel we've been overstepping, and we can even talk to them about identifying a local therapist or support group. Therapy is a normal and healthy coping strategy for life, and many of our friends have probably used the services of a therapist at some point in their own adult journey. They'd likely be happy to help us in finding a safe space to get the additional support we need. Friends cannot be expected to meet *all* of our emotional needs, but they can certainly be there for us as we figure out how to find our way back to a more healthy relationship and life balance.

FRIENDING EXERCISES:

1. How can you skip the programmed "good" and instead answer with a more honest response when asked about your day? Use the space below to start practicing those more authentic replies.

2. Can you think of someone in your life who could use some support and solidarity in the kicking of their "trash cans?"

3. Is it time to call in some additional reinforcements? Do you need to consider adding a therapist or support group to your current coping strategy? If yes, use the space below to clarify a plan, including the role of your friends.

Go Ahead, Air That Laundry: Making a Commitment to Truth Telling

If we are going to be authentic people in authentic friendships, we are going to have to get comfortable with the giving and receiving of truth. This goes beyond a commitment to exchanging our programmed "goods" with more authentic responses about our lives. This is about permission to forego entrenched messages that tell us that honesty and vulnerability are "weak," and debunking the lie that we must keep our "dirty laundry" deeply buried if we want to be loved and accepted. This is about realizing that meaningful, enduring relationships encourage and celebrate the telling of our truth.

When we choose, in any given situation, to tell the truth instead of pretending, we help move us all one step closer to our goal of collective authenticity. When we text a close friend to ask for support after being passed over for a job, we all take a step. When we post on social media about our bad days, as well as our good days, we take another step. When we are brave enough to share with others about our struggle with depression, or open up about childhood abuse, or humbly confess a misstep, we all make a leap. When we offer empathy and support to someone else who is brave enough to do any of the above, we aid in perpetuating the cycle of authenticity. And so it goes, on and on, until the "airing of laundry" is the new norm, and we all start to feel more secure in the sharing of our real selves with each other.

When one of my clients, Eve, first started her therapy process, we had to spend a lot of time reexamining her internalized messages from childhood. She had grown-up in a home where emotional truth-telling was seen as "weakness." Being vulnerable, admitting that you were struggling, and asking for help were seen as merely frivolous. She was expected to "suck it up" and to "pull herself up by her bootstraps." She understood, as an adult, how these messages could be damaging to a child and acknowledged that she would never accept such teachings for her own children. Nonetheless, she struggled to let herself off the hook for these long-held expectations.

With time, Eve was able to consider these unhealthy messages in the context in which she learned them. She acknowledged that her family of origin was dysfunctional, as she shared about how she was expected to be completely self-sufficient from a very young age, even expected to find her own food and other living necessities. But most heartbreaking,

Eve shared that her childhood was almost completely void of emotional support from her family. Eventually, Eve was able to acknowledge that her forced self-sufficiency from such a young age had not served her well relationally. She had done what she needed to do to survive her childhood, but she'd also allowed that survival mindset to dictate most of her intimate relationships since then. She struggled to be authentic, to be vulnerable. It was hard for her to ask for help, and she didn't let people get too close. She spent most of her life pretending to be "okay."

Through our weekly sessions, Eve developed a growing awareness of the toxicity of her internalized childhood messages. She was eventually able to shed some of her unhealthy, entrenched thoughts and make a commitment to telling the truth in her relationships—leading to a newfound sense of freedom. With this, she was able to—perhaps for the first time in her life—ask for help when she was struggling and accept care when it was offered. It was a life changing transition, and we celebrated it well.

Eve was just one of many of my dear clients to wrestle with these negative internalized associations about emotional truth-telling. The more social research I've done, the more aware I am that this struggle is also still quite pervasive in our society as a whole. It always makes me sad when I encounter it, as I have come to believe that one of the most important things we can do when we are hurting is to reach out to others for their support, because we desperately need each other's care.

I do want to take a moment here to acknowledge that being a truth-teller can have its ups and downs. There are still many people who subscribe to the "you don't air your dirty laundry in public" mentality. And, while I think I understand where and why these types of mentalities were born, I can honestly say that I have never seen them lead to increased connectedness amongst people. So, if you do encounter resistance in your attempts at truth-telling, do not be discouraged. Simply stay your course, and tell your truth.

My challenge for us, then, is to overcome our barriers to truth-telling, so we can invest in deep, connected relationships with other people. This will not be an easy process, as it will require that we address the root issues that have kept us stuck. It will require that we process and resolve the painful parts of our relationship history that have resulted in fear, shame, and mistrust. And, it will require that we choose to trust again. While it will inevitably take some time, and some difficult work, I believe that the investment is worthwhile, as there is no pathway to intimate friendships that does include a commitment to telling each other the truth.

FRIENDING EXERCISES:

1. What are some specific truths you need to share with your friends?

2. What negative internalized messages do you need to relinquish in order to be able to fully embrace authenticity in your life and your relationships?

The Storytellers and the Space Holders: Trusting Each Other with Our Real Stories

We all need safe places to share our stories. We have each had a variety of experiences throughout our lives, and we need people in our lives who can be trusted with all of the messy and wonderful details—people who will be present and caring, who will not judge us, and who will hold space for us. People who will stand in solidarity with us.

We also need to be this person for others. We need to be the friend who can provide care and space, who can listen and empathize. We need to own our personal stories enough to be able to offer empathy to a friend who is walking a difficult road—a road which we may have already traversed. We need to be able to *give* and *receive* this gift of honest storytelling. This is foundational to authenticity and to meaningful, enduring friendships.

As I have been increasingly committed to authenticity in my relationships, I have been so heartened by the reciprocity I have encountered. In fact, last year, as I was coming to terms with the fact that my physical and emotional health were going to necessitate a stepping away from my private practice for a while, I confided in a colleague about my mounting fear and doubt about the looming change. I will always remember her response. She offered me an authentic moment of solidarity. She shared with equal vulnerability about her own struggles, fears, and doubts. And let me tell you, it was friendship magic—exactly what I needed the most in that tender moment. This sweet colleague reminded me that I was not alone in my struggles. She normalized my experience, and she offered me solidarity, and in doing so, she released me from my shame. What a precious gift.

I wish this brand of authenticity and vulnerability came more easily to us all. I understand, however, that we've all experienced disappointment and hurt in our lives, and those experiences can make it difficult to offer our friends access to the deepest parts of our hearts and souls. However, part of the challenge of this chapter (and this book) is for us to pursue the healing we need to be able to engage with our people in more open and honest ways.

While I would recommend that we share our stories organically, we should be mindful of environments and circumstances that may affect our sharing process. For instance, it might be difficult to have a deep sharing session in a loud or distraction-ridden location. It might also be difficult to bare our souls when we or our friends are overly tired. So, if we know our friend is not a morning person, it might be better to reserve a sharing session for a time when they might be more mentally and emotionally available—or at least until after they've had their first cup of coffee. It is important that we be conscious about sharing our stories in ways and environments that are conducive to us feeling heard.

I also want to take a moment to issue a caution here: Not everyone is a safe person. Some people have been deeply wounded, and they have not yet done their healing work. They cannot hear or hold the intimate parts of our story with care. We will probably recognize an instinctual holding back with some people—let's give ourselves permission to trust those instincts.

Beyond our instincts, we can also give ourselves permission to take a step back in a friendship when someone is consistently disinterested, dismissive, or demeaning. Because, while I still advocate for authenticity in all relationships, I do not advocate for deep sharing in emotionally unsafe relationships or for consistently putting ourselves in a position to be wounded. If someone is not ready to provide the care and reciprocity we need in the sharing of our story, it is always okay to utilize healthy boundaries to ensure our emotional safety.

If you have realized, or are now realizing that you have shared the intimate parts of your story with someone who is not capable of providing the attention and care you and your story deserve, it is okay to start implementing necessary boundaries *now*. You are always allowed to share as much or as little of yourself and your story as you feel comfortable. You don't have to be vulnerable with someone who is not ready or is simply not interested. It is always okay to take a step back and to reallocate that emotional energy into more healthy friendships.

FRIENDING EXERCISES:

1. Is there someone in your life that you could trust with an important part of your story that you have been hesitant to share? Jot down their name and create a plan for sharing.

2. Is there someone you could support in the telling of their story? How can you best provide a listening ear?

3. Have you been sharing your story with people who cannot provide the care and support you need? If yes, is it time to create better boundaries in those relationships? Use the space below to clarify a path towards healthier friendships.

BEING AFFIRMING

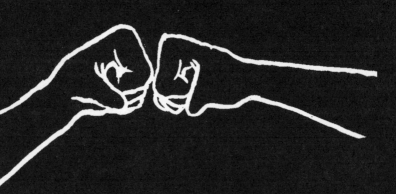

I am hopeful that we have all experienced an abundance of affirmation in our lives, that we have all had friends who have been able to compliment and celebrate us well. I am also hopeful that we have been people who felt comfortable offering affirmation to others, that we have taken full advantage of opportunities to express our admiration and affection for our people. If not, I hope this chapter will help in moving us all closer to experiencing and extending this affirmation in our relationships, especially when our friends might need it the most.

A couple of years ago, I had an incredibly unpleasant run-in with an adult neighbor that left me reeling. After the initial interaction, I also received an equally disturbing letter delivered right to my doorstep. It was full of insults about my weight, which had nothing to do with the initial unpleasantness, but was assumedly a way for this person to communicate their anger towards me. It included lines like, "Your face is so overly fat that you no longer look healthy," and "Stop eating all of the food." It was signed off with, "Fat, fat, fat. Bad girl. No cookies for you." To say that I felt shocked as I read the letter would be an understatement.

Now, I am confident that most of you know that writing and delivering a letter like this one is never okay, no matter what. Not ever. And thus, this chapter is less about the inappropriate letter and more about the boatloads of affirmation I received from my friends after receiving this letter—affirmation that I desperately needed, even more than I realized in the moment.

". . . You are one of the most beautiful people I know, outside and in . . ."

". . . You are sincerely one of the most stunning women I have ever met . . ."

". . . You are loved and admired by gazillions of people . . ."

". . . You are wonderful . . . And I was thinking earlier today that you are such a fun, nice, effervescent, beautiful, and wonderful person . . ."

While the awful letter I received was certainly an unexpected blow to my self-esteem, these simple words of affirmation from my people were a welcome balm and a needed reminder that I was loved and appreciated by those I valued most. I hope they will serve as a reminder to us all of the importance of affirmation to and from our friends, especially during our "no cookies for you" moments in life.

And so, this will be the challenge of the coming chapter: To encourage and equip us all in the intentional giving and receiving of affirmation, to be people capable of noticing when our friends need us, and to be people capable of verbalizing genuine encouragement and solidarity when we notice.

Bedroom Dressers, Bathroom Mirrors, and Car Dashboards: The Importance of Self-Affirmation

I am sure that most of you have heard the saying that it is impossible to pour from an empty cup. While it's not a perfect analogy, there is certainly merit to its premise. If we don't know how to be kind and compassionate with ourselves, it is difficult—if not impossible—to authentically extend this brand of care to our friends. To this end, we all need to become more comfortable with self-care, and as part of that practice, self-affirmation.

My client, Karen, had started coming to therapy to address her increasingly prohibitive anxiety and depression, which were negatively interfering with her relationships with friends and family. She had become overwhelmed by life, isolated, and stuck, and she was finding it impossible to reach out for help or to connect with her people at all. As we talked more about her life circumstances and her relationship history, it became clear that Karen was devastatingly insecure. She had internalized a lifetime of negative messages from parents, peers, and partners, and she now believed these messages to be true.

As Karen and I continued our regular sessions, we were both increasingly aware that at the core of her relationship issues was her lack of ego strength, and that, if she was going to be healthy enough to risk being open and vulnerable with other people, she was first going to need to heal and nurture herself. She was going to have to learn to like and accept herself, before she could believe that other people would like and accept her. We both understood that this would be a process, and luckily, Karen was a willing and engaged participant.

We started this healing process by having Karen do a simple exercise. I asked her to work with me to identify ten things that she really liked about herself. We had to push past a lifetime of internalized lies to get to the truth about who Karen was, and what amazing things she had to contribute to the world around her. This was no easy task, so we took our time, and with support and encouragement, Karen was able to compose a list that made her proud.

Karen wrote down this self-affirmation list, took it home from our session, and immediately made three copies. She then chose three prominent places to post her lists, places that would ensure that she see them every day. She opted to post one on the dresser in her bedroom, one on her bathroom mirror, and one on her car's dashboard. We agreed that she would read the lists, out loud, at least three to four times per day for the following month. She was a model client, and she went above and beyond our agreed upon terms.

When I saw her at our next appointment, a month after making the affirmation list, Karen seemed like a different person. She was smiling and showing her natural humor, which I had not experienced up to that point in our process together. She spoke more positively, her body language was more confident, and perhaps most importantly, she reported spending more time with friends and family. It was obvious that the self-affirmation list had its intended effect, and I was thrilled for Karen, as she was happy and hopeful about the future. This outcome reminded again how powerful it is when we choose to focus on our strengths and gifts, versus allowing our old mental tapes to continue to perpetuate self-doubt and paralyzing shame.

If you can relate to Karen's struggle with insecurity, you are certainly not alone. Most of us have spent our fair share of time in the struggle. Whether this is due to the voice of a critical parent constantly playing and replaying in our minds, or the relentless ridicule of peers that we can't seem to shake, or unhealthy societal messages that we have internalized, or unrealistic expectations that we created for ourselves that have rendered us stuck in a perpetual cycle of disappointment and shame, most of us have wrestled with self-esteem and self-acceptance at some point in our journeys. And many of us have had these issues affect our relationships in some way, whether in some relatively minor way, like an unexpected jealousy response to a dear friend's happy news, or something more major, like finding ourselves increasingly isolated due to a looming fear of further rejection and hurt.

Listen, we all *want* to be happy for everyone's happiness, and that's such a worthy and beautiful goal. But, if we are struggling with pervasive insecurity, it is going to be really, *really* hard to do. It takes a lot of emotional reserves to watch a friend celebrate her engagement while we curse Match.com for yet another horrible date. Or to watch a friend get offered their dream job, while we mourn yet another terrible job interview. Or to see pictures on social media of someone taking a dream vacation, while we can barely scrape together enough money for the rent. If we are going to be able to genuinely affirm our friends and celebrate their happy news with them, while keeping envy and jealousy at bay, we are going to need to take some steps to deal with our insecurities.

There are a number of strategies for managing our insecurities in healthy ways. One strategy—the self-affirmation list mentioned above—helps us consistently focus our attention on the things we like the most about ourselves. By using our self-affirmation lists multiple times per day for at least a month, this tool can help us internalize new, positive messages about ourselves. And, as some of you may already know, research indicates that any behavior repeated consistently for 28 days becomes a habit. So, in the same way, if we commit to consistently affirming ourselves for this period of time, new habits related to self-appreciation and ego strength can be created.

Another strategy for managing insecurity is through thought replacement. Similar to affirmation lists, thought replacement is the process of consistently replacing negative internalized messages about ourselves with positive messages. This means that every time we realize that we are using shaming thoughts or language about ourselves, we consciously choose to stop and replace.

If you need some help in this process, I've got you:

Negative Message: I am fat and ugly.

Replacement: My body is healthy and strong, and I have beautiful eyes and a kick ass smile.

Negative Message: I am stupid and will never be able to achieve my goals.

Replacement: I am capable and determined, and I will reach my goals if I purpose to do so.

Negative Message: No one will ever love me, and I will end up alone.

Replacement: I have a great sense of humor, a generous spirit, and a tender heart, and I choose to offer these unique relationship gifts to others, because I am capable of loving and being loved.

Any self-affirmation habits we create that are aimed at addressing, versus repressing, our insecurities will aid in our goal of consistently offering ourselves and our people the affirmation we all so need and deserve.

FRIENDING EXERCISES:

1. List the ten best things about you. Then, make copies of this list and post them in prominent places, so you can remind yourself of your unique awesomeness at least a few times every day for the coming month.

2.   If you know that you struggle with self-affirmation, take some time today to think about why. What negative messages from your past are you allowing to control your thoughts about your self-worth?

3.   Utilize the space below to confront some of your negative internalized messages, and then replace them with positive truths about yourself.

Doctor Cool Boots: Becoming "Fluent" in Affirmation

I dream of a world where affirmation flows easily and often from our mouths. Where we are purposefully on the lookout for chances to extend this goodness to others. Where compliments are the norm, and everyone gives and receives them on the regular. Where we notice someone's beautiful smile or sense of humor or stylish outfit, and actually say it *out loud*. Because I have come to understand that the affirmations we speak can dramatically change someone's day—our own included—and can have a contagious effect on the world. It can spread from one giver to one recipient, from that recipient to another recipient. And so it continues.

As with most practices, we will become more fluent in Affirmation the more we give and receive it. It's like a foreign language in that way. When you initially start speaking a different language, it might feel awkward or uncomfortable. But, with time and practice, it becomes easier and easier, until we can speak more naturally and confidently. I find that the same is true of Affirmation. If we commit to the practice, we will find it becoming more organic with each use.

Earlier this year, I made a visit to my local Urgent Care, and my assigned doctor of the day was a bit terse. Professional, but . . . not friendly *at all*. I am not one who responds well to feeling completely emotionally detached from my care providers, especially when my physical well-being feels compromised by the detachment, so I knew I needed to turn things around STAT. Then, the proverbial clouds parted and I noticed that my doctor was wearing the coolest boots—not necessarily Urgent Care appropriate, but *super* cool—so, I complimented him.

And, *oh my goodness*, the entire tone of our interaction changed instantaneously. He started showing off his boots like a proud school boy. He even strutted around the room (I kid you not!) to show them off more, all the while sporting this huge smile, which I had not seen up to that point. It changed my entire visit moving forward, both in regards to how he interacted with me and how thorough he was in his treatment planning. Now, I'm not going to pass judgment—at least not at the moment—on whether or not it was fair for me to be responsible for offering affirmation to my doctor when I was the one who was sick. But, I will tell you confidently that I don't regret a thing.

This situation at Urgent Care was such a potent reminder of the power of affirmation in changing the dynamics of an interaction. I had become detached from my affirmation language, as I was dealing with a long list of my own stuff at the time of this visit. But I was incredibly grateful for the opportunity to recommit to noticing the beauty in those around me, and to speaking it—even if the opportunity did not necessarily come in the way I might have anticipated or desired.

If the idea of practicing your Affirmation Language with strangers sends you into a panic, then I would recommend that you start the process with friends and family. It makes sense that we would feel more comfortable making a commitment to regularly complimenting the people closest to us before branching out to local bank tellers and baristas and doctors with cool boots. So, start wherever you are most comfortable and grow your affirmation skills from there.

If you are someone who struggles to find appropriate affirmations in the moment, let me offer a little help:

> *"I really admire how you share so openly and honestly about your thoughts and feelings when we are all together. I think it makes us all feel more comfortable being open in response."*

> *"Thank you for contributing so thoughtfully and intelligently to conversations that can sometimes be tricky to negotiate."*

> *"You do such a great job of finding and sharing joy with the people around you."*

> *"I am so grateful for your amazing sense of humor. After the difficult time I've been having lately, it is so refreshing."*

> *"Wow, you are such a rockstar. Going back to school while also working and volunteering cannot be easy. You inspire me."*

Healthy affirmations are about noticing and verbalizing our friends' admirable attributes and accomplishments. So, if you are struggling to find an affirmation for someone, ask yourself, "What do I most admire about my friend?" And then, *tell them*.

Now let's also take a quick moment to address the brand of "affirmations" we should avoid with our friends (or anyone):

"Damn, you look hot in those pants."

Okay, really, any variation of this should be avoided, especially in different gender friendships. Objectification is not a healthy affirmation. And being a creep under the guise of being "affirming" is awkward at best and offensive at worst. So, skip it, or replace it with one of the healthy affirmations suggested above.

Additionally, genuine affirmations require that we be sincere. Fake or shallow compliments are pretty easy to recognize, and they do not tend to grow connectedness amongst friends. Sarcasm in the giving or receiving process is also a no-no. And backhanded compliments . . . *just don't.* If we really want to make healthy affirmation a foundational tenet of our friendships, let's be conscientious in the process of finding and communicating the best in our people.

Now, if *accepting* compliments is the panic inducer for you, then I would recommend taking some time to reflect on why. Why is it difficult to embrace positive feedback from others? Do you need to take some time to work on internalizing some new messages about yourself? If yes, you are not alone. And it is never too late. In the meantime, I would simply challenge you to make a commitment to sitting with the compliments you receive and allowing yourself to hear them. Allowing them to just be. And then, to reply with a "thank you," versus a deflection or denial. As with most things, the more you practice this skill, the more comfortable you will be with it.

One of the things I love the most about my beloved T-Town crew is that we regularly practice giving and receiving affirmation with each other. We can spend an entire evening together, laughing and playing and complimenting the dickens out of each other, and still . . . I can not think of one get-together in the last few years that was not followed (usually later that same evening) by a round of post-togetherness affirmations—about how wonderful the food was, or how lovely the decorations were, or how much fun we all had together, or how excited we are about our next shindig. It's such a joy to send and receive those messages, and it certainly lends itself to all of us being more comfortable with offering affirmation outside of our intimate circle, as well.

FRIENDING EXERCISES:

1. Do you speak fluent Affirmation? If no, what barriers are standing in your way, and how can you work to remove them?

2. In the coming week, write down a list of affirmations about your friends. Then, next week, commit to sharing at least one of these compliments with its appropriate recipient. The following week, increase that number to two. And, as you grow more comfortable, extend this practice to people outside your group of friends, as well.

3. Can you think of a healthy affirmation you received lately? How did it make you feel?

Making Those Deposits:
Affirmation as Friendship
"Currency"

While I would never advocate for making our friendships purely transactional in nature, I have found that a "bank account" tool can be highly effective in helping us focus more purposeful attention on making affirmation deposits in our friendship accounts. You see, much like a bank account, we reap the most relationship benefits when we commit to making regular "deposits," ensuring that these deposits outweigh whatever "withdrawals" we might be taking from our friendships. I have found that remaining committed to this process and being conscious of our friendship "balances" is key to ensuring that our relationships continue to thrive.

So, how do we make deposits in our friendships? Well, simply stated, whenever we contribute positively, we are putting money in the bank. When we sincerely congratulate our friend on a promotion, compliment a flattering, new outfit or haircut, send an email of appreciation for a friend's consistent support and encouragement, or simply call or text out of the blue to let someone know we're thinking of them. Alternatively, we take withdrawals from our friendships when we choose attitudes or behaviors that could negatively impact the relationship. When we say harsh words in a moment of frustration, gossip about a friend's separation from their partner, opt to be overly critical of a friend's new endeavor, or even when we initiate a difficult conversation with limited funds in our relationship account.

If we are to make a commitment to having meaningful, enduring friendships, we will need to ensure that we are making more deposits in our relationships than we are taking withdrawals. In fact, research indicates that healthy relationships have a five to one ratio of positive to negative.[10] This means that for every withdrawal we take from a friendship, we need to make five deposits to find our way back to relationship health. So, if for some reason we realize that we have a friendship account that has been existing with a less than ideal ratio, it is important that we make purposeful deposits as quickly and as regularly as possible. I would recommend that if we find that our friendship accounts are overdrawn, that we commit to *only* making deposits until the friendship finds its way to more balanced territory.

Ultimately, the key to keeping our friendship accounts consistently balanced really comes down to a commitment to being aware. If we pay attention, we can usually tell when a friendship is feeling distant or strained. When we realize that

10 Kyle Benson, "The Magic Relationship Ratio, According to Science," *The Gottman Institute: The Gottman Relationship Blog*, October 2017.

this is happening, we can start thinking about how to best invest in the relationship to get it back to a place of health and connectedness. If you need some "deposit" ideas, feel free to borrow from the list above, but I am guessing you all might know better than I do about how best to make deposits in your specific friendships.

As with most things, if we realize that a friendship is consistently in the "red," it is time for a conversation. This might be as simple as sharing the bank account analogy with our friends and inviting them to join us in making more intentional deposits. Sometimes awareness can help change the dynamic of a relationship. By acknowledging that our friendship is in unhealthy territory, we can commit to working together to correct the deficit and transition to a season of friendship health and satisfaction, hopefully with many positive returns.

FRIENDING EXERCISES:

1. Do you have a friendship that is currently operating in the red? If yes, jot down one thing that you can do today to make a significant deposit in that relationship.

2. Are there friendships in your life that are due for a deposit? Take a moment now to list the names of those friends and commit some time this coming week to get some affirmation currency in that account.

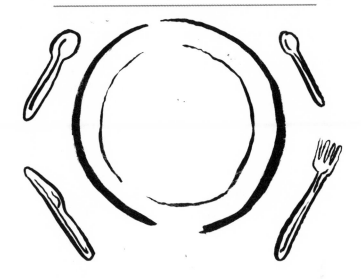

Making Space at the Table: Overcoming Our Instincts to Compete

S ome of you have heard the saying that "comparison is the thief of joy. " This rings true for me—*really, really true*. Comparing ourselves to each other: "She is so much farther along in her career than I am." Competing with each other: "I *will* finish the marathon with a faster time than him. He cannot win at everything." Feeling jealous of each other's accomplishments: "She doesn't have to worry about anything. She always succeeds at whatever she does, while I am over here struggling all the time. It's not fair." If any of this sounds familiar, welcome to being a human being. We've all been there, but these comparison habits can certainly bring out the worst in us. They can steal our contentment, compromise our motivation, and if not wrangled, they can ultimately derail us and our relationships. So, if we are to have healthy friendships, we will need to learn to be aware of these habits and to ensure that we are managing them.

As I was finally settling into the completion of this book, after many years of keeping it on the back burner, I noticed other writers releasing their own books on similar topics. These were writers I respected and admired, and I must admit, I allowed myself to be overcome by self doubt, asking questions like, "What more do I have to contribute on the topic of relationships?" And thinking, "I can't compare to his humor and wit." "I haven't done as much research as she has." "I should accept that this is not meant to be." With every single comparison and self-criticism, I became more and more paralyzed in my own writing process. In fact, I almost allowed those competitive voices in my head to shut it all down completely.

I have since read most of the books that I had allowed to plague me with insecurity, and I can tell you confidently . . . they are all beautifully written. And delightful. And worthy of all of the praise they have received. I have unreservedly recommended them to all of the readers in my life. But, I can also tell you confidently that . . . those books are not my book. They were not written from my unique perspective. And I believe, like never before, that there is still room for my input on some of our shared topics.

I also think this experience offered me a fresh perspective on how we can more universally combat our instincts to compete with each other. It might be as simple as a commitment to making space, because there is room at the table for us all. We can all contribute something unique to the conversations that are being had around us, because we are all unique. No one else has my story or experiences. And no one else has yours. So, let's share our stories, and let's pursue our dreams. And let's cheer other people on as they share and pursue theirs.

Now, when I say that this is a "simple" commitment, I don't mean to imply that this will come easily for all of us. We will have to make a choice to combat our instincts to compete. And keep making that choice. It may even be helpful to have a script we use to accomplish this desired change in perspective. Maybe something like:

> *"I don't have to compete with other people. I have a story that is uniquely my own. And I can choose to be happy for others, as they are creating and sharing a story that is uniquely theirs."*

As with all behavior modification, this consistent choosing of one response over another can eventually create new habits related to the way we think about and respond to our competitive impulses. So, who's up for the modifying of unhelpful behaviors? Who will join me in this goal of transitioning from competition to collective cheerleading?

Now that we've talked a bit about curbing our competitive impulses towards others, let's also take a minute to address our response to a friend who might be jealous of *us*. Perhaps a friend who is consistently using competitive language or trying to make us look bad in front of other friends. If we notice this pattern of unhealthy behavior, as with most issues, it is best to initiate a conversation. We could start by offering the observation to our friend. We could say:

> *"I have really enjoyed our friendship the last few years. Lately, though, I've noticed that you often seem to be*

hostile toward me, poking at me when we have get-togethers and trying to discredit me whenever you have the opportunity. I am not sure if you are aware that you are doing this, but it has started to make me dread any time that I know we might be together. Can we talk about what's going on and try to find a path to a more healthy relationship dynamic?"

As acknowledged throughout this book, I believe healthy communication about friendship issues is always the right decision, even when these conversations might be uncomfortable.

Let's remember that comparison and competition just don't have a lot to offer us. In fact, they usually serve to get us stuck in an unhealthy cycle, either of thinking our lives and choices are better than someone else's *or* thinking that our lives and choices suck in comparison to someone else's. Neither provides much positive, healthy momentum. So, let's try to squash this ugly thing whenever we realize that it has snuck its way back into our heads. And, as we squash it, let's choose to replace it—replace it with confidence about what we have to contribute, with appreciation for what others have to contribute, with enthusiastic celebration for us all. I promise this fresh commitment will not only lead to more joy in our lives, but it will also lead to happier and healthier friendships.

FRIENDING EXERCISES:

1. Is there someone in your life who you find yourself regularly competing with? If yes, write out a script for combating that instinct when it arises next.

2. Is there something that you have wanted to do in your life that you continue to sideline for fear of being compared to someone else? If yes, outline the project details below and start making some purposeful steps toward achieving that goal.

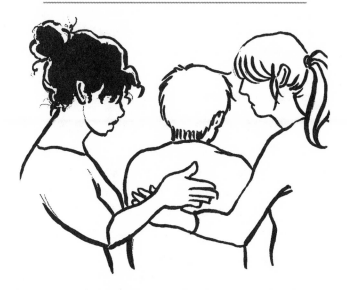

Me, Too: Affirmation as a Pathway to Collective Empowerment

I have come to believe that affirmation can take many forms. And, in these forms, it not only has the power to affect us and our friends, but also to affect our society as a whole. When we commit to collective empowerment, we open the doors for connection and change on a much grander scale. Collective empowerment means that we stand-by and stand-up for those who are on the front lines of our shared battles for social justice, human dignity, and equality. This means that we support each other and encourage each other's bravery, that our own empowerment leads to the empowerment of others. It means that we are in this thing together, that we need each other.

As most of you know, there has been a recent growing movement to stop the cycle of sexual inequality, sexual harassment, and sexual assault, which are far too prevalent in our society. The #MeToo and #TimesUp movements have brought increased awareness to how widespread these issues are, and it has been heartening to see people from so many different backgrounds coming together to take a stand and participate in a purposeful movement toward meaningful change.

Last year, I watched Oprah use her platform at an awards ceremony to speak passionately to these issues and to rally us all to join her in taking a stand. "For too long," she said, "women have not been heard or believed if they dare speak truth to men in power. But their time is up." It was a moving and empowering speech, and it offered hope to many victims, including myself and many of my friends and clients. The responses of solidarity following were equally heartening, and I was so encouraged that this kind of movement was happening in my lifetime.

Since then, I have had ongoing conversations with friends about our own stories of harassment, assault, and discrimination. I have been reminded anew of how many people in my own social circles have been affected. Friends who have been passed over for professional opportunities, because they refused to have sex with their bosses; friends who have been sexually assaulted by co-workers and lost their jobs when they came forward; friends who have survived decades of inappropriate sexual comments and have endured ongoing blame because, "Why would she wear such a tight top if she didn't want that kind of attention?" So, while not all of my friends agree with every part of the #MeToo and #TimesUp movements, we do all agree that the important conversations they have brought to the forefront of our collective consciousness are essential for our healing and empowerment.

I wholeheartedly believe that we can continue to find common ground to create positive momentum toward much needed social change, but this will require that we believe each other, that we validate each other, and that we support each other. And, as Oprah so eloquently said, "What I know for sure is that speaking your truth is the most powerful tool *we* have." I love that she chose "we" instead of "you," because that seems like an important distinction. Our stories, while our own, provide collective empowerment for others in the sharing of theirs, and all of our stories together become a tidal wave that cannot be easily ignored.

FRIENDING EXERCISES:

1. Have you ever experienced collective empowerment? Perhaps you've been to a rally for a cause that is dear to your heart? Or to a book reading by your favorite author on an issue that you are passionate about? How did this experience make you feel?

2. How can you use your Affirmation Language and unique platform to aid the cause of collective empowerment?

3. Are you a person who encourages and empowers those who are on the front lines of the important issues of our time? Use the space below to think about why or why not, and if you might want to reconsider your contribution.

BEING ASSERTIVE

This chapter may be the one most of us have either dreaded or looked forward to the most, as it seems a majority of us could use some help with being more assertive in our relationships—with consistently and clearly communicating our needs and wants. Whether we have been on the receiving end of assertiveness done wrong, or we have internalized the message that "nice people don't confront," Many of us have some negative associations around the concept of assertiveness. I know I certainly do. The more I study healthy relationships, however, the more I realize that healthy assertiveness is necessary for meaningful, enduring friendships. So, that is the goal of this chapter—to help us all in accepting and assimilating assertiveness in our lives.

I have a pretty bad memory, as most of my closest friends and family will attest. On rare occasions, this has served me well, but it has turned out to be more of a burden than an asset over the years, especially in my intimate relationships.

My friend Tracey, on the other hand, has an incredible memory. Tracey remembers a lot of our initial interactions in college, which were rather hurtful to her. I was a different person at that time of my life, as I had not done much of my healing work. I could be pretty harsh, often sarcastic, definitely opinionated, and much less compassionate. I said and did things then that I would never say or do now. Things that I have forgotten, but things that many friends on the receiving end have not. Tracey was among these friends.

A few years ago, some of my girlfriends from college were able to cement a reunion. This was a small miracle, as we are all busy people. So, it goes without saying that we were all excited as we counted down the days to finally being together. When we arrived at the restaurant, it was all hugs and laughs and reminiscing. That is, until things took a sharp turn. You see, Tracey could no longer hold in her hurt, and it all came spilling out over our fancy dinner, as she confronted me about a long list of offenses she'd collected over the early years of our friendship. I remembered very little of what she was sharing, so I felt blindsided and angry. I became defensive and tearful and eventually retreated to the restaurant bathroom. A few other friends came to retrieve me, and we processed for a while before I ultimately decided to offer a simple apology to Tracey before collecting my things and leaving, not knowing if Tracey and I would ever have a healthy friendship.

Some time passed before Tracey or I were ready to talk, but we did eventually schedule a time to meet. The three hours we spent together in her car on that spring afternoon brought us both insight and compassion that had long been missing from our relationship. I realized that while we had always been polite to each other, we had never been completely honest, and thus we could never enjoy a deeper connection. We had both been doing a lot of pretending in the relationship, so it felt incredibly healing to be completely authentic with each other, for perhaps the first time in our friendship. While the catalyst for this shift was initially painful (and perhaps poorly timed), I am genuinely glad that Tracey decided to be assertive. It was the reset we desperately needed, and it convinced me anew of the importance of assertiveness, even when the process may be a bit bumpy.

And so, this sets the framework for the coming chapter—a hope that we will all be able to better understand and embrace the importance of being assertive in our friendships. That we will ask for what we need. That we will admit when we've been hurt. That we will seek resolution to the issues that might hinder, derail, or destroy the connectedness we all need and deserve.

The Bad Rap: Clarifying the Difference Between Assertive and Aggressive

It seems there may be some confusion about what it means to be assertive in our friendships, so let's jump right in. At its core, assertiveness is about being honest. It's about communicating when a friend disappoints or offends us, about asking for what we want and need, about becoming comfortable with healthy boundaries, and about contributing our real thoughts and feelings to our conversations. Assertiveness is about standing up for ourselves to ensure that we feel heard, understood, and respected. Ultimately, being assertive is about making a commitment to creating and maintaining friendships that invite and embrace authenticity.

To clarify further, being assertive is *not* about being aggressive. It's not about being rude or critical; it's not about manipulating our friends; and it's certainly not about attacking or demeaning our people. Assertiveness never seeks to use harm—emotional or physical—to get what we want and need. The intended result of assertiveness is to protect and respect one's self, and, ultimately, one's friendships. It seeks to grow and preserve, not damage and destroy.

I must admit that I have been discouraged at times seeing people using the badge of "assertiveness" as an excuse to be mean. I cringe every time I hear phrases like, "I'm just keeping it real," when in fact, someone is just being a jerk. There are far too many of us who are being mean under the guise of being assertive, and this only serves to undermine our collective understanding and acceptance of this important concept. If we cannot contribute respectfully to our relationships and must resort to bullying, mocking, name calling, or being disrespectful, in general, then we are not actually practicing assertiveness. We are practicing asshattery. And it's important that we realize the difference. Because, as mentioned above, the "line" can sometimes be difficult to discern, especially when emotions are involved.

So, for those of us who might still feel unclear on where the "line" is, I wanted to provide us with some concrete examples:

Assertive: While I respect your opinion, I have a different perspective that I'd love to share.

Asshattery: That is the stupidest thing I have ever heard! You are an idiot! Do you live in a cave or something?! (rude, belittling, immature)

Assertive: I wanted to let you know that your comment at the party last night really hurt my feelings and made me feel embarrassed in front of our other friends.

Asshattery: Why do you always have to be such a bitch to me every time we're around other people?! You really are the worst friend on the planet! (rude, aggressive, name calling)

Assertive: I have been feeling a little neglected lately. Could we schedule a time to hangout this coming week?

Asshattery: Clearly you don't value our friendship as much as I do, so I guess I'll have to make some new friends! (immature, manipulative, extremist)

More recently, I had a client who had endured a childhood filled with emotional and physical abuse by his parents. John had been dragged by his hair, thrown against walls, and punched in his face on a regular basis. Even more harmful, he had been constantly told that he was unwanted and unloved by the very people who were supposed to want and love him the most. Understandably, this toxic childhood experience led John to adopt a survival mentality, where his main priority in any relationship was to protect himself.

John's internalized messages from his childhood left him believing that he had to be constantly armored and ready for a looming attack. Whenever he sensed that he might be emotionally unsafe—which was more often than not—John could be quite aggressive (often confusing this with being assertive) in an effort to protect himself from further pain. He was well known in his social circles for yelling insults at people when he felt misunderstood or demeaned in a conversation, and we would even resort to physical threats and posturing when he felt his intimidating language was not sufficient for making him feel fully in control of a situation.

As you might suspect, all of John's emotional armor and instinctual aggressiveness made it incredibly difficult for him to make and keep healthy friendships, especially since he didn't initially realize that his reactions were crossing the "line." As we worked together, and John started to address issues from his childhood, he realized that he needed to make changes. We decided to start that process by having him internalize some new truths about himself, utilizing some of the tools shared earlier in the book (namely self-affirmation lists and replacement). As John was internalizing that he was smart, funny, capable, and deserving of healthy friendships, he was simultaneously learning to internalize new truths about relationships—mainly that there were good, healthy, people in the world, capable of providing genuine care and concern for him.

As his internalized messages changed, John became increasingly able to distinguish the line between assertive and aggressive, finding himself more and more on the right side of that line. He was able to verbalize his needs and wants in his relationships, without resorting to aggression or intimidation. He was able to tolerate differences of opinion without becoming overly defensive or belligerent, and he was able to receive assertive feedback from others without immediately defaulting to shame and corresponding anger. Best of all, though, with this growth, John began to create increasingly healthy friendship connections, which made my counselor heart smile.

I share John's story not only to demonstrate the difference between assertive and aggressive, but also as encouragement—no matter where we have been, or where we currently are in our process, we can choose to do assertive in a healthy way. We can figure out how to negotiate the line between assertive and aggressive, and we can cultivate friendships that celebrate being on the right side of that line. I believe in us.

FRIENDING EXERCISES:

1. After reading this section, what do you think are the main differences between assertive and aggressive? Use the space below to jot down some ideas about what you can do to ensure that you stay on the "right" side of the line in your friendships.

2. Can you think of a time when you have been on the "wrong" side of the assertive/aggressive line? How did that feel? How you can avoid finding yourself in that space in the future?

Passive No More: Relinquishing Our Assertiveness Avoidance

Most of my clients realize at some point in their therapy process that they need help being more assertive in their relationships—as I am convinced most people do. You see, many of them, like many of us, don't feel like they can or should speak up for themselves, and thus, they often unintentionally acquiesce into living passive lives. Unfortunately, I have found that long-term patterns of passivity usually result in some combination of insecurity, bitterness, and resentment, because none of us can be truly content in our relationships if we are not giving ourselves permission to be real and honest about our thoughts and feelings.

A couple of years ago, I realized that a good friend was no longer engaging with my posts on social media, after a few years of regular and enthusiastic engagement. I tried to ignore it. I tried to let it go. I tried to reallocate my energy elsewhere. I tried to passively resolve the issue within myself. But as I saw him regularly engaging with other mutual friends, I felt myself growing more and more offended and agitated. I simultaneously felt embarrassed that a lack of "likes" and "comments" from a friend would elicit such a strong and growing emotional response. But there it was—I felt hurt.

After much consideration and months of passivity, I finally reached out to my friend and asked him if there was some reason why he was no longer engaging with me on social media. He admitted that he was going through a rough season and was finding my happy posts about my happy life with my happy job and my happy marriage difficult to see on a regular basis, as he was struggling with his own singleness and dissatisfaction with his job. I reminded him that my life was not full of happiness all of the time, which he knew, but he shared that this awareness alone had not assuaged his struggle. As we talked more, I was grateful to better understand where he was coming from. We had a really healthy dialogue about our friendship and the role of social media in our friendship, and we agreed that we would be more assertive if situations like this occurred in the future, to avoid any unnecessary ongoing disconnection.

While my decision to be assertive with my friend about his social media disengagement provided a happy outcome, I must admit to you something that you probably already know—not all assertiveness produces the same positive results. Sometimes we will choose to be assertive and our friend on the receiving end might respond negatively to the confrontation. They might get defensive, or angry, or simply deflect. They might turn the tables to avoid taking responsibility for hurting us, or they might seem to hear us in the moment, but the hearing does not result in resolution or changed behavior. So, choosing to be assertive and to forego passivity in our friendships means that we need to be prepared that not everyone will be mature or healthy enough to deal with this honesty.

I still remember when I found out that my husband and I were not invited to a dear friend's milestone birthday celebration. We were part of an intimate group of friends who spent a lot of time together, and we had invited Ed and his wife to many of our celebrations over the previous few years. We considered them like family. Needless to say, we were shocked when another friend from our group asked if we would like to carpool to Ed's party the following weekend, and we realized over the course of a dozen text messages that we had not been invited. We were understandably confused and hurt.

That evening, after some contemplation, I decided to be assertive and call Ed's wife to communicate our hurt at being excluded, since she was the party planner. She issued an apology, but she did not feel the need to give much of an explanation for her decision, nor did she take that opportunity to extend an invitation to the party. My decision to be assertive in this scenario did not produce my desired outcome, and sadly, that was to be a major turning point in the relationship.

Some people might question my decision to be assertive in this situation. Some might say, "Wouldn't it be better to ignore this than to potentially derail a close friendship over a party?" And sure, I certainly could have chosen the passive route. I could have pretended that I didn't know about the party. I could have pretended that it was not a big deal to be excluded from the invite list. I could have pretended that I wasn't hurt and that things were fine. But do you notice the theme? *Pretending. The epitome of passivity.*

The older I get and the longer I research relationships, the less I believe in passivity as a viable long term option for friendships. It does not encourage authenticity, and thus, it will never lead to real connectedness. Admittedly, deciding to be assertive in this situation did not lead to a storybook happy ending, but it did ensure that I had been honest with myself and with those I had considered to be close friends. You see, assertiveness is sometimes about ensuring that we are cultivating real relationships, and ensuring that the people we allow access to the most intimate parts of our life are committed to the same.

If you realize, like I did, that you need to have an assertive conversation with one of your friends, I would like to offer a sample script (which we will cover in even more detail in the next section of the book):

You could start by saying:

"I really enjoy our friendship and count you among my closest friends."

Then, depending on your specific assertive message, you could say something like:

"Because I value our relationship, I feel like I need to let you know that <fill in the blank with the set of circumstances that you need to address> made me feel

<fill in the blank with the emotions the circumstances elicited for you>."

Then, end with a simple:

"I would really like to understand where you are coming from, and if there's anything we can do to resolve the situation in a way that feels good for both of us (or at least helps us avoid any misunderstanding or hurt in the future)."

This may seem like an incredibly forward approach for some of you, especially if you have been relegated to living passively for most of your life. But, as you have probably already discerned, I wholeheartedly believe that open and honest communication is the best chance we have for establishing healthy, long term connections.

We can sometimes fall into the trap of thinking that passivity is akin to kindness, goodness, and likability. And let's be really honest—most of us desperately want to be liked, even if it means relinquishing part of our authentic selves in the process. Let me offer a caution, however, that there is a high price to be paid for long term passivity. In addition to the potential for insecurity, resentment, and bitterness, passivity can ultimately lead to anxiety and depression, along with a whole host of other intrapersonal and interpersonal issues. When we feel like we can't be genuine, and begin to live in conflict with ourselves, our minds and bodies will inevitably respond negatively. So, let's spend some more time thinking about how we can best combat our passive tendencies and invest in our relationships more honestly.

FRIENDING EXERCISES:

1. What is your greatest fear about being more assertive in your friendships? How can you actively work to overcome that fear?

2. Do you find yourself regularly choosing passivity? If so, take some time this week to think about and write down the potential reasons why, and what steps you can take to become more comfortable with healthy assertiveness.

3. Do you need to invite a friend to join you in combating your passive tendencies? Maybe a friend who could also benefit from some accountability on this issue? If yes, use the space below to clarify a plan.

How to Make an Assertive Sandwich: The "Sandwich" Approach to Healthy Assertiveness

When I spoke at a women's conference a few years ago, I wanted to ensure that I left attendees with some tangible resources they could take home with them to utilize in their friendships. So, when I received post-conference feedback from the event planners, I was thrilled to hear that there was actually one simple tool that had really seemed to "stick." One very simple analogy about healthy confrontation that conference goers had continued to talk about weeks after my speaking engagement. And that was the often-recycled "sandwich."

The "sandwich" is based on the relatively simple concept that if we find ourselves in a situation where we need to confront a friend, there is a way to do that which aims to preserve, versus damage, the relationship. Best of all, this confrontation "sandwich" can be made in 3 easy steps.

1. We start with a *bottom piece of bread*: This is the part of the process where we initiate the confrontation by offering some initial affirmation to our friend to assure them that we come in peace. This is where we set the stage for a healthy and productive conversation that seeks to preserve and enhance the relationship, so it is important that this part of the process be warm and sincere.

   Example: *"Karen, you are such a valued friend, and I love spending quality time with you."*

2. Then, we add *the meat* (or other delicious sandwich fillings): This is the part of the process where we communicate the offense, the thing we most need our friend to hear (and usually the thing we find most difficult or intimidating to say).

   Example: *"Lately, it seems like you have been preoccupied with your new job. We have made multiple dates over the last few months, and you have cancelled all of them at the last-minute. While I want to be understanding and gracious, I also want*

> *to feel like our relationship is still a priority in your life."*

3. And finally, we add the *top piece of bread*: This is the part of the process where we do a healthy wrap-up by offering another affirmation to our friend as a sign of our commitment to the ongoing health of the relationship.

> Example: *"Karen, again, you know that I adore you, and I think the feeling is mutual. I think we both want to maintain our friendship, so I really look forward to working together to make that happen, as I have really missed spending time with you lately."*

Even if we are nervous about taking the first steps toward being more assertive in our friendships, this "sandwich" approach is a pretty simple way to try assertiveness on for size. The steps in this process are easy to remember, and they allow for affirmation before and after the confrontation. Best of all, the process can be as short or long as we want it to be. I find that the more comfortable people get with the process (and the idea of being assertive, in general), the longer and more authentic these conversations tend to become. So, let's give ourselves permission to start short and sweet and grow the process with time.

If we find ourselves on the receiving, versus the initiating, end of a "sandwich," I certainly hope that we will listen and really hear what is being communicated by our friend. I hope we will attempt to receive the message being shared with an open mind and heart, will make every effort to manage our potential defensiveness, and will be gracious. If we need to respond, I hope we will do so in a similarly healthy way, maybe creating our own "sandwich" as part of that process.

There are many issues that can arise in our friendships, because everyone is different, and we are complicated and flawed people. So, whether the necessary confrontation is about a pattern of miscommunication or increasingly different interests, or it's about something more serious like ongoing boundary violations or other blatant disrespect, we can all benefit from extra tools for addressing the problems that might occur in our relationships over time. And, if done right, this particular tool—the "sandwich"—can be an incredibly healthy addition, especially if assertiveness has not been previously employed in our relationships. So, I encourage you to try it out, and then share it with others who might need a similar resource for practicing assertiveness in their own lives.

FRIENDING EXERCISES:

1. Have you been harboring some unexpressed disappointment or frustration toward a friend? Clarify your feelings below and then commit to sharing a "sandwich" with your friend sometime this week.

2. Is there any part of this process that seems especially intimidating to you? Why?

BEING ACCEPTING

We all like the idea of acceptance. It has a warm, fuzzy feeling to it, doesn't it? Something we could all cheerlead for? Something we could all rally behind? That is, until we are asked to offer acceptance to a friend with whom we have a major difference of opinion. That's when acceptance can get dicey—not quite so warm and fuzzy. And, that's when we might be tempted to haul out the judgment and beat our friends over the head with it until they "come around" to our way of thinking. Eek. We've all been "that" person at some point in our journey. And, thus, this chapter is for us.

When I was a freshman in high school, my family had to make a cross-country move due to a job change for my mother. So, we packed up our van, and we moved from an urban area in South Carolina to a very rural area in Washington State. I was devastated by the change. And I was afraid. We were moving from a place I knew and was settled, to a place where I would know no one. *Not one single soul.*

I tried to hope for the best, but on my first day at my teeny, tiny new school in the teeny, tiny town of Belfair, WA, I quickly realized that my concerns were completely valid. I *did not* fit in. I had huge, permed hair, preppy clothes, and a thick Southern accent. I was a *freak* in this tiny, rural town where everyone had known each other since birth, and flannel was the fashion staple of choice.

I don't remember a lot about those first few months in that strange place, but I remember the first person who really made an effort to reach out to me. Her name was Missy. She invited me to a parade, even with my big hair and my thick accent, and that parade was to be the first of *many* friendship outings together. Over the following months and years, Missy and I would share countless adventures. We stayed close through high school, and both of us decided to attend the same college, where we would have even more adventures, most of them supremely fun, and more than a few involving attempts to get the attention of completely oblivious boys.

When I went to Missouri for grad school, Missy was the only friend from home to visit me there. When I found myself in need of a roommate after returning home from grad school, she joined me on that adventure, as well. And she even agreed to be my Maid of Honor at my wedding in Mexico when I finally found and married my handsome husband.

But our relationship began to change after I was married. I don't remember all of the reasons why we started to grow apart. I guess some shifts were inevitable, since our friendship had been defined to that point by the two of us adventuring through the world together as single ladies, and I would no longer be a single lady. But even as our friendship was experiencing some strain due to all of the changes in our relationship dynamic, and we both grew in different ways and found ourselves with increasingly different interests, we were able to maintain a relationship. It has not always been easy, but we have remained committed to making space for each other and all of our differences. We have been able to adjust some of our expectations, and we have come to more fully accept each other and our new dynamic.

At any point in the past several years Missy and I could have called it quits. We could have decided that all the changes and differences were too much. Both of us have other good friends, and so we both would have been okay. But, I'm glad we decided not to go that route. No one has known me as long or as well as Missy has, and I would rather find acceptance for each other and our differences than lose such a longstanding, meaningful bond.

And so, that will be the challenge of this chapter. To encourage and equip us all in finding ways of offering acceptance to our friends, especially when we are negotiating our differences. Whether those differences be minor league or major league, I believe that with commitment and some additional tools we can all manage to make room for our friends and their unique thoughts, beliefs, and life courses.

Lemons, Matching Sweater Vests, and Bad Romances: Allowing Our Friends to Chart Their Own Courses

Acceptance is essential in a meaningful, enduring friendship. We all need to feel that our people make space for us and want to have our backs. That we can count on them to embrace us, even when we might choose life paths that they don't fully understand. We have to feel safe to be ourselves, and we have to be able to offer the same to our friends in return.

Sometimes our friends might choose paths that we don't get. Maybe they decide to give up a successful job to pursue an elusive dream, or maybe they choose to move far away to pursue a fresh start. Maybe they insist on trying every fad diet that makes its way onto the scene. Sometimes our friends might even choose paths that we think are unwise. Maybe they decide to invest their life savings in a seemingly shady business venture, or they choose to end their marriage abruptly, or they start coping with life stressors by drinking on a more regular basis. Whatever the circumstances though, our friends will undoubtedly make decisions about their lives that we would not choose for ourselves. And we will have to decide how to be there for them as they negotiate these decisions and subsequent outcomes.

I know that I have certainly made my fair share of life decisions which have left friends scratching their heads. In high school, I decided to use all of my allotted "car money" to buy an absolute lemon—against the advice of all of my friends who actually had legitimate car knowledge—because it had a "cute" sunroof. In college, I decided to be in a traveling drama/singing group. We wore matching sweater vests. Enough said. For grad school, I decided to move from Seattle to *Missouri*, far from all of my closest friends and . . . all the good coffee. In my late twenties, I decided to date a guy who *all of my friends* knew did not treat me right, even after concerns were clearly communicated with me *many* times. In my thirties, I decided to leave a successful job to pursue a volunteer position in South America, where there were more than a few safety concerns at the time. Upon my return, I decided on another round of dysfunction with the guy who all of my friends knew was bad for me. Then, in my forties, after finally finding my sweet partner, we decided to publicly announce our decision not to have children—to the shock of more than a few people. And the list could go on . . . and on . . . and on.

While some of these head scratchers were obviously more confounding to my friends than others, I have been consistently *blown away* again and again by how my people have rallied behind me as I have stumbled through the ups and downs of life. Though they didn't always understand all of my decisions, and communicated these concerns at times, my friends still showed-up with unconditional love and care. They still agreed to listen to me vent when my decisions ended badly, as they knew they would. They still picked me up from the side of the road when my lemon of a car overheated for the millionth time. They still hung out with me in public as I sported my nifty sweater vest, following my painful acapella performances. They still sent me care packages across the country with all the good coffee from Seattle. They still supported me financially (and stored my earthly goods) as I embarked on my volunteer adventures, and they still hugged me when I cried, because my heart was broken *again*. They accepted my confounding decisions, and they cheered for me, over and over, despite my trips and falls. They helped me get back up and dust myself off. And they sent me back into the world knowing that they'd always have my back. I'm so grateful for their support and acceptance.

We can all think of our own examples of friends showing up with unconditional love and acceptance when we came to them with decisions we knew they might not understand. And we can all think of examples of the opposite, as well—times when friends did not offer us the support we needed. Times when friends might have harshly judged us or even outright rejected us. If you have known the pain of the latter, I am sorry. I have known some of that judgment myself, and it stings. My hope is that we will use both these positive and negative experiences as motivation to provide our friends in the here and now with the support we most needed and wanted in our own journeys.

Now, I want to take a moment to clarify what I am *not* saying here. I am not advocating that we encourage decisions by our friends that are toxic to them or others. I do not believe that we should throw our eager support behind a friend who is abusing alcohol or drugs, or a friend who has chosen to be in an ongoing abusive relationship, or a friend who is involved in perpetuating prejudice or hate. There are times when acceptance is *not* the answer, and I am trusting us to know where the line is on this one. If we are not sure, here's a good question to help: "Are the decisions that my friend is making willfully hurting them or someone else?" If the answer is "yes," it's okay to confront the situation or call for reinforcements. If the answer is "no," it might be time to figure out how best to offer acceptance to our friend, as they chart their own unique course.

We all need and deserve friends who will allow us space to chart our own courses even when those courses may traverse some potentially rocky terrain. And, I truly hope that if we haven't found those friends yet, that we can. And I hope we can work toward *being* that friend, work toward offering love and acceptance for our people, especially when they need it the most.

FRIENDING EXERCISES:

1. Do you have a friend who has chosen a life path that you've struggled to understand? Why are you struggling, and how might you reach out to better understand and offer support?

2. Do you need to invite friends to join you in pursuing a dream, knowing that they may not fully understand? If yes, how might you go about this?

Red Light, Green Light: Disagreeing with our Friends Without Judgment

In our quest to offer acceptance to our people, we will inevitably be met with roadblocks of different kinds. When our friends vote for the "wrong" political candidate, or chooses to date the "wrong" person, or say the "wrong" thing when we come to them for advice, we will probably be tempted to haul out the judgement. And while we should be aware that some wrong choices by our friends could be indicators of a potentially unhealthy friendship dynamic, we should also be aware that mere disagreement is not grounds to dissolve a relationship. And thus, we must learn to address our judgmental impulses.

To be fair, this struggle is pretty universal. I don't know anyone personally (or professionally) who has not had to get their judgmental attitude in check at one time or another. And social media has made this all the more difficult, hasn't it? It seems we feel far more comfortable being judgmental from behind a screen; we say things we would never dare if we were face-to-face with our friends. And so, its seems more important than ever that we be able to communicate with each other with respect, even when we disagree.

Please don't misunderstand, I am not advocating that we don't stand up to bullies or confront injustice. I am a *huge* proponent of both. Sometimes we need to use our assertive skills to protect someone or to speak truth to something. This chapter is more about how we communicate with someone with an opposing, but not unjust, viewpoint.

We can disagree—even vehemently—while keeping the doors of communication open. This does require that we be aware and capable of managing our triggers, that we remain respectful, and that we continue to remind ourselves that the person on the other end of the argument is a fellow human being, and often a friend. I know this might seem quite a feat when we are debating an issue that is important to both individuals, but I believe we can do it.

For those of us who might be thinking, "That sounds great. But, how?" I have come bearing gifts. <insert drum roll here> I present you all with . . . *The Stop Light!* This approach is a relatively simple method for thinking through the reasons we are feeling judgemental in any given situation to ensure that we don't get derailed.

The red light means stop. The first step in this process is being able to identify when we are becoming emotionally flooded; when we are struggling to manage strong feelings that a situation might induce, and thus, we become less capable of managing judgmental impulses toward our friends. When we realize that we are approaching this emotional "intersection," we can use the "red light" as a reminder to *stop*. This is the most important step in the process—to actually stop before we say or do something we'll regret. Sometimes the "stop" will last a few seconds, and sometimes the "stop" will last for significantly longer. But regardless of the duration of the "stop," when we are overwhelmed by unhealthy impulses, this is a crucial first step.

The yellow light means caution. The next step in this process is to actually think before proceeding cautiously with any course of action. This is our moment to really consider the "why" behind our judgmental impulses toward our friends. Why am I feeling triggered right now? Why do I feel so strongly about this issue? Why do I feel like my opinion is the only "right" opinion? This pause allows us a moment to consider a path forward that is not rooted in judgment. And, it ensures that we are taking the time necessary to work through all of the things that may have lead us to this place. This is also a great time to consider the consequences of acting on our impulses, so we can decide whether this course is really worth the relationship "clean-up" that might be necessary later. Once we have worked through this invaluable step, we are usually ready to proceed, with caution, to the next.

The green light means go. This final step in the process is usually the easiest, as we've already done the hard work of actually stopping and thinking. The "green light," then, provides us the opportunity to put into action what we've worked out in the previous step. This is where we (hopefully) decide to communicate our thoughts and emotions to our friends in a healthier, less judgmental way, conducive to a respectful dialogue. If we are unsure about how to do this, we could borrow from the "sandwich" approach discussed in the previous chapter. And then, we can decide with our friends on a mutually agreeable resolution to whatever situation prompted our emotional response in the first place, before formulating a plan to ensure that we can manage future disagreements without judgement.

That's it. That's The Stop Light. As someone whose biggest friendship regrets would have been avoided if I had stopped, thought through my "whys," and proceeded on a path more conducive to connection and health, I am hopeful that this resource will provide us all with a tangible way to avoid any further regrets of this nature. <insert green light here>

FRIENDING EXERCISES:

1. Have you been overly judgmental of a friend in a recent interaction? If yes, take some time this week to think through the interaction again, using the Stop Light approach. And, if necessary, construct and issue an apology.

2. Is there any step in this approach that you think might be unusually difficult for you? If yes, identify it in the space below and commit to practicing it, so you are more comfortable utilizing this resource if the need arises in the future.

Relationship Lessons from an Adolescent Client: Offering Acceptance without Agreement

It is important to acknowledge that we can offer acceptance to our friends without offering agreement. I have many friends (and many clients) from many different backgrounds and with many different worldviews, and I have found that it is not overly difficult to offer respect and validation for other people's ideas, even if we might disagree with them. We must just purpose to do so.

This "purposing" can best be accomplished when we make a commitment to curiosity in our friendships. When we can ask questions. When we can listen. When we can understand that losing a meaningful connection in order to win an argument is counterproductive to the goal of healthy relationships. Yes, this process does require some additional awareness—and sometimes a lot of humility—on our parts, but we can all benefit from some extra doses of both.

I had an adolescent client a few years ago who insisted on talking about his disdain for Christianity as part of almost every one of our initial sessions. You see, Chris knew I was Christian, and he was testing me to see if I would continue to offer him unconditional positive regard, even if he strongly (and very vocally) disagreed with my religious beliefs. Because of the nature of our professional relationship, it was only appropriate that I offer my client room in our process for his worldview (and testing), as this is essential to building a healthy therapeutic alliance. And, as is often the case, in exchange for this space and acceptance, my adolescent client offered me his trust.

Chris and I would go on to have a few years of meaningful and productive sessions. He grew a lot through our process together, and I felt proud when he successfully transitioned to the next season of his life. As I reflect on our success now, I recognize how foundational unconditional acceptance is for building trust and intimacy. While Chris was a client, and not a friend, this lesson translates to all of our relationships. If we can purpose to offer our people respect and acceptance for their thoughts and feelings, then we can earn the right to go deeper. The foundation of trust will be there. And with trust, there can be intimacy. With intimacy, there can be genuine connection.

In addition to the lessons about acceptance and trust, this process with my adolescent client also highlights the importance of having people in our lives who might not look and think and act exactly like us. Perhaps friends who grew up in different cultures. Friends who work in different fields. Friends who have different interests. Friends who have had different life experiences. I wholeheartedly believe that our lives are enriched by friends who offer us different perspectives and challenge us in different ways. Making a commitment to investing in diverse friendships makes us better humans, and it lends itself to us being more successful in our attempts to offer acceptance more universally as we learn and grow, and hopefully become more aware and compassionate people.

FRIENDING EXERCISES:

1. Can you think of a friend who has been pushing your buttons lately? If yes, brainstorm how the dynamic might change if you were to offer them unconditional positive regard (instead of judgment, irritation, or disdain).

2. What is something you could do today to foster a greater sense of acceptance in your friendships, especially with your friends who may think about the world differently than you do?

3. Do you realize that you need more diversity in your friend group? If yes, how might you go about creating those connections?

Permission Granted: Adhering to Healthy Boundaries

While I wholeheartedly believe that acceptance is one of the foundational tenets of a meaningful, enduring friendship, I also believe that it is always okay, and sometimes necessary, to utilize boundaries in our relationships. It is okay to say "no" when we need to. It is okay to protect our emotional and physical well being. It is okay to take a step back. And, I believe all of this can be done without judgment or disdain to our friend on the receiving end. We can offer genuine compassion and empathy to our friends even as we might be taking a step away from the situation.

There are many reasons why we might find it necessary to employ *firm* boundaries in a friendship. Maybe a friend refuses to pursue the help and healing they need for a chronic addiction issue, and this behavior has resulted in them lying to us and putting us in compromising situations. Maybe a friend continues to return to an abusive romantic partner, and expects us to intervene when things go sideways in their relationship. Maybe a friend is often disrespectful or mean to us, and thus, leaves us feeling emotionally unsafe. Or maybe a friend just refuses to provide reciprocal care and concern for us, even after we bring the need to their attention. When our friends are engaging in behaviors that are unhealthy or potentially dangerous, it is *always* okay to utilize firm boundaries. It is okay to limit spending time in situations that make us uncomfortable or compromise our physical or emotional safety. We can still care for our friends without continuing our active participation in an unhealthy relationship dynamic. This can be a tricky balancing act, but I believe it's possible.

If we are unsure how to employ healthy, firm boundaries in these types of situations, I would like to offer a script:

> *"While I genuinely care for you and want the best for you, it is clear that this friendship is not currently healthy. I cannot change you. That is your work to do. But, I need to take a step back for now to take care of myself."*

Conversations like this are never easy, but sometimes they are necessary to preserve our own emotional health. Depending on the friendship dynamic, this "step back" could be for a predetermined amount of time, or could be dependent on our friend's healing process, or could be more permanent in nature. Regardless, if we need to communicate a more firm boundary in an unhealthy friendship as an act of self care, let's give ourselves permission to do so.

Let me also take a moment to acknowledge that there are a plethora of situations that can arise in our friendships that are less serious than those shared above, but that still justify using boundaries. Maybe a friend has a habit of interrupting us while we're talking. Maybe a friend insists on calling us during work hours, even after we've reminded them numerous times that we can't take personal calls at the office. Maybe a friend expects that we attend every fundraising event that they host, and makes us feel guilty when we cannot meet their expectations. Maybe a friend teases us in a way that makes us feel uncomfortable. Whatever the situation, it is *always* okay to use boundaries whenever we feel unheard, ignored, or disrespected.

If we are unsure how to employ healthy boundaries in these types of situations, I would like to offer an additional script:

> *"While I genuinely care for you and value our friendship, I am feeling unheard. I would appreciate it if you could be more aware about <insert behavior that is causing issues in the relationship dynamic>, as this behavior makes me feel <insert appropriate emotion>. I would really like to have this issue resolved, so we can get our friendship back to a place of mutual enjoyment."*

These conversations may be awkward at first, but as you might have already guessed, I believe that honest communication is the best chance we have of creating meaningful, enduring friendships.

My client Steve and I had been working together for quite a while when he started sharing more honestly about his friendship with Kyle. He and Kyle had been friends for over a decade, and since they both had experienced difficulty finding and keeping other adult friends, they had spent a lot of time together. While they did have a lot in common, they could also be incredibly disrespectful to each other, often calling each other names and engaging in immature chiding about their expanding waistlines and diminishing hairlines. And, unfortunately, over time, this became the norm for the relationship.

As Steve continued to open up about his friendship with Kyle in our sessions, he shared that he had grown increasingly uncomfortable with the dysfunctional dynamic they had created in the relationship. He admitted that he was embarrassed about what he had contributed to the dysfunction, but he also felt stuck. Having been a regular contributor to the immature banter and blatant disrespectful tone of the friendship, he did not feel like it would be "fair" to expect that dynamic to change now, after so many years.

While I knew that this dynamic would be difficult to change, I also knew that the current dynamic was not healthy for Steve or Kyle, and had not been, maybe ever. So, Steve and I began talking more seriously about the need for a healthy confrontation. We discussed the importance of finding the right time and space to talk, and we practiced using the "sandwich" approach in the hopes that having a script would help keep the conversation from heading into defensive territory.

When Steve finally did confront his friend, the conversation was uncomfortable. Kyle was quick to point out that Steve was as much to blame for their current relationship dynamic as he was. Steve was able to own his part of the dysfunction, but the dialogue still did not end well. Kyle was not sure he wanted to invest in changing and healing the friendship, and he left their meeting rather abruptly, without any clear resolution.

When we processed this interaction at our next session, I was able to normalize the experience for Steve. We were able to celebrate the step taken and plan for what was to come. We discussed the fact that Kyle might ultimately decide to end the friendship, but we also discussed that he may decide to re-engage after having some time to process further. Steve felt comfortable with either outcome, though he was sad about the prospect of losing his friendship with Kyle altogether.

Kyle did eventually reach out to Steve, communicating a desire to work on the friendship. They had some seemingly healthy and promising phone conversations over the course of the next few weeks. But, unfortunately, the next time they were together in person, Kyle defaulted to loudly making fun of Steve's weight in a very public place, making him feel incredibly stung and discouraged about the possibility of real, lasting change in the friendship.

As Steve and I processed this situation further, he ultimately realized that he and Kyle needed a more long term break from each other. So, he made a date to meet with Kyle that week to communicate his intention to take a step back for the time being. While it was certainly sad, Steve shared that he also felt an overwhelming sense of relief, to finally be committing more seriously to friendships that were healthy and mutually satisfying, versus accepting a friendship dynamic that was contrary to his current relationship goals.

While the situation above might not be a friendship-ender for you personally, I think it is important that we remember that there may be times in a friendship where we can't make the relationship work. We might try and try, only to find that we can't get on the same page. The list of potential reasons will be different for different friendships, but regardless, it is okay to take a step away if a relationship cannot find its way back to mutually enjoyable territory. We are allowed to utilize boundaries in any relationship that is unsatisfying, unhealthy, or unsafe. If you have a friendship like this and have been needing someone to give you this permission . . . *Permission granted.*

FRIENDING EXERCISES:

1. Do you currently have a friendship in your life that has become unhealthy? If yes, have you talked to your friend about your concerns? If no, write out a strategy for communicating your concerns this coming week.

2. Do you have a friend that you have confronted numerous times, but now realize you need to release (for now)? If yes, brainstorm that process in the space provided, including a potential timeframe for communicating your decision.

Confessions of a Bad Friend: The Role of Forgiveness in our Friendships

We have all been the "bad friend" at some point in our relationship journeys. At least, I know I have. I missed a dear friend's wedding because I was overcome with my own pain at still being single. *Selfish.* I missed another close friend's milestone 40th birthday bash because I was careless in the scheduling of a family vacation and didn't realize the conflict until it was too late. *Thoughtless.* And, I missed another friend's graduation, because I overexerted myself the day before the event on completely insignificant tasks and could not get my body to cooperate on her important day. *Misprioritization.* And, the list goes on. I have let my friends down more times than I care to admit, and thus, found myself in need of forgiveness just as many times.

Forgiveness is an incredibly important component of any friendship. The decision to offer grace for a friend's misstep, to relinquish our resentment over a friend's mistake. Meaningful, enduring friendships require that we have the ability to ask for forgiveness, as well as offer it. However, part of our decision to embrace forgiveness includes a decision to offer often undeserved grace to our friends. This is no easy ask, especially when we've been disappointed or hurt by them.

A choice to forgive will also require us to accept the hurt that we have sustained from our friend's selfish or thoughtless or misprioritized choices. Not acceptance that the hurt caused was okay, but instead acceptance that it cannot be changed. Acceptance that the only way forward in the relationship is through an honest resolution process.

I also believe that offering grace to our friends usually includes some honesty about the disappointment and hurt we ourselves have caused others. Acknowledgement that as flawed human beings no one has negotiated their friendships perfectly. When we spend some time really considering our collective messiness and imperfection, I am hopeful that we can all realize how invaluable forgiveness is in creating and sustaining deep friendship connections.

Now, I want to take a moment here to acknowledge that there are different brands of hurt that friends can cause in our lives. There are "**scratches.**" These might be sustained by a friend's careless words in a moment of frustration, or an unnecessary lie. Then there are deeper "**cuts.**" These might be sustained from a friend's choice to distance themselves from our lives without explanation or to withhold an important invitation. Finally, there are the incredibly painful, potentially relationally lethal "**flesh wounds**." These might be sustained by a friend's decision to have an affair with our partner or a serious physical injury sustained from an angry encounter. Obviously, different brands of pain will require different responses, and the more painful the offense, the longer the necessary healing process. While I believe that forgiveness is ultimately the right decision in most situations, as it releases us from the burden of collecting and carrying our hurts around with us long term, I do not believe that anyone should be forced into a process before they are ready. And, I strongly believe that "flesh wounds" require us to work through our potential anger, bargaining, and depression (i.e. a healthy grief process) before an authentic forgiveness process can even be considered.

Additionally, I have come to earnestly believe that to forgive is not to forget. We are not a forgetting people, at least not when it comes to the hurts we've sustained at the hands of our friends. Forgiveness, then, requires that we extend grace, while fully knowing that we will carry the memories of serious hurts with us even after the process is complete. Forgiving a friend does not mean that the hurt is magically erased. Hurts that we sustain become part of our story. They often stay with us. So, if we choose the forgiveness route, we should do so with this information in mind.

Finally, I do not believe that forgiveness asks us to continue in chronically unhealthy relationships. To forgive a friend is not to accept a relationship dynamic that has become toxic. Or to pretend that someone is capable of meeting our needs, if we realize that they are not. It does not require that we continue on a path that leads to further hurt, or that we live our lives pretending. We will have choices to make about whether or not we continue in friendships with those who have hurt us. And while I certainly believe that the restoration of some friendships is possible and completely worthwhile, I do not believe that the forgiveness process requires that all friendships be restored or continued.

So, as we strive to better understand and implement forgiveness in our friendships, I would like to offer a couple of guides for helping negotiate these sometimes complex processes. First, I want to offer a simple guide for issuing a healthy apology:

Step One: Share your feelings about the hurt you caused.

Example: *I am genuinely sorry that I hurt you and caused damage to our friendship. I feel really sad knowing that I did something that created a barrier in our relationship.*

Step Two: Take responsibility (avoid excuses).

Example: *I know that my actions were not conducive to fostering connection and trust, and I regret that.*

Step Three: Ask for forgiveness and make reparations.

Example: *I would like to ask for your forgiveness and see if there is anything I can do to get us back to healthy friendship territory.*

Issuing an apology when we've hurt our friends is an important part of the forgiveness process, as it gives our friends the *opportunity* to forgive us. Saying "I'm sorry," taking responsibility for our actions, and offering reparations paves the way for the potential healing and restoration of the friendship.

In addition to the guide above, I would also like to offer a guide for initiating a forgiveness process. This process is helpful when we find that our friends do not issue the apologies we desire (usually because they don't realize that they have caused us hurt), but we recognize that we need to communicate the offense and pursue a forgiveness process to bring about some necessary resolution.

Step One: Set a specific time and place to talk with our friend(s) about the hurt they have caused us, making a commitment to discuss only the issue at hand and to being open and honest about our thoughts and feelings throughout the process.

Step Two: Ensure that we can be fully present in the conversation by removing any potential distractions and focusing all of our emotional energy on getting the clarity we might need to be able to move forward.

Step Three: Clearly and concretely share our reasons for pursuing a forgiveness process, and what we might be expecting from the process.

If our friend did not realize that they had caused us hurt, they may be quick to communicate their remorse and issue an apology at this stage in the process. We should allow this to unfold organically, especially if we sense that sentiments being shared are authentic.

Step Four: If we are ready, this would be the appropriate time for extending forgiveness to our friend. If we have received a heartfelt apology, this part of the process will feel incredibly satisfying. If for some reason, however, our friend does not feel they owe us an apology, we will have to decide whether to extend forgiveness to them anyway, with the goal of unburdening ourselves from any further negative emotional responses related to this issue, or whether to put the conversation on hold.

Once we have extended forgiveness to our friend, we can commit to moving forward with our lives and embracing the freedom that this process is intended to offer us. This may include a decision to re-engage in the friendship if a sincere apology was received, and we feel that a healthy and meaningful relationship dynamic can be restored, or this may be the part of the process where we decide to take a step away from the relationship. Let's give ourselves permission to do whatever is most healthy for us.

In a perfect world, we would never hurt our friends, and they would never hurt us. But since we don't live in a perfect world, and none of us are perfect friends, we might find ourselves in need of forgiveness. If we realize we've caused a friend hurt, I hope that we will apologize as soon as possible. If we don't realize it, and our friend finds the courage to bring their hurt to us, I hope we will own whatever we might have contributed to their hurt and apologize then. And, I hope that we will all embrace authentic forgiveness as an essential part of the meaningful, enduring friendships we are striving to create.

FRIENDING EXERCISES:

1. Do you owe a friend an apology? If yes, formulate a plan.

2. Do you need an apology from a friend? If yes, draft a script for sharing your hurt with them. And when you are ready, use the guide above to pursue the closure you need.

3. Have you ever received forgiveness from a friend? How did it make you feel? What would it mean to make a commitment to that practice in your ongoing friendships?

CONCLUSION

SAYING GOODBYE TO LONELINESS

I am hopeful that this book, and its friendship-making and keeping criteria, has provided some valuable insight and tools for creating the meaningful, enduring relationships we all need and deserve in our lives. I hope these resources will further ensure that we no longer have to live in fear of loneliness and instead feel increasingly confident in our friendship-making abilities. Since research suggests that 70% of our overall happiness comes from our relationships, I wholeheartedly believe that a commitment to understanding and assimilating this information is important and worthwhile.

As I mentioned at the start of this book (and referenced throughout), I have a close group of friends who I adore—my faithful T-town crew. I have countless memories with this group of people—happy, sad, excited, disappointed, angry. They've been there through it all. And, when I think about how we have maintained our connections throughout the years, I come back to my five criteria for making and keeping meaningful, enduring friendships.

We have committed to being *available* for each other. We show up. Physically. Mentally. Emotionally. Spiritually. We issue invitations to coffee chats and birthday parties and graduations and celebratory dinners. We attempt to limit distractions when we are together, unless they are of the hysterically funny brand. We listen to each other and support each other. And we regularly pray for each other.

We have committed to being *authentic* with one another. We are honest and vulnerable. We share our real stories—the good, the bad, and most enjoyably, the really, really funny. We accept each other's messiness. Try to make room for each other's shortcomings. And we always attempt to avoid pretending to be anything or anyone other than what and who we are.

We have committed to being *affirming* of each other. In fact, we can be a bit ridiculous on this front. We regularly give each other over-the-top compliments about new haircuts and outfits and recipes and party decor and . . . you name it, we affirm it. We loudly and enthusiastically cheerlead for each other as we pursue our different educational, professional, and relational goals, and we try not to allow comparison or competition to interfere with our earnest support of each other.

We have committed to being *assertive* with each other. We are open and honest about our thoughts and opinions while trying to remain on the "right" side of the line. We don't shy away from necessary conversations about our needs and desires. We don't harbor resentments about disappointments, but instead address issues as they arise. We provide safety and space for each other and regularly encourage and empower one another toward greater confidence in utilizing our individual and collective voices.

Finally, we have committed to being *accepting* of each other. We extend grace to each other for our differences, and believe me, we have more than our fair share. We allow one another to pursue our own courses, even if we might not always understand them. We try to always keep our judgemental impulses in check and commit to talking through issues that have the potential to get us stuck. And we forgive each other well.

We all make mistakes in the friendship process. We are all flawed and messy and selfish and easily distracted. We all have a lot on our plates. And we all have our own blind spots and biases. In short, while we adore each other, and we earnestly and purposefully try to be the best friends we can be, we are not perfect. No friend or friend group is. So, we trade the elusive concept of perfection for the real and meaningful relationships we have created. They are gloriously imperfect. And, highly recommended.

ACKNOWLEDGEMENTS

To my amazing publishing team at Microcosm: Thank you for making this seemingly elusive dream a reality! I am so grateful that you took a chance on a new author and invested the countless hours necessary to make this book the very best version of itself. You have been patient and kind and honest with me throughout this process, and I am so glad that my book journey brought me to you, as I cannot imagine doing this first writing venture with anyone else.

To Cecilia Granata: Thank you for the beautiful cover art! They say not to judge a book by its cover, but in this instance, I think an exception is warranted.

To Karen Quintana: Thank you for being the first person to recognize the potential in this project! Whether you realized it or not, your words of affirmation brought this book to life.

To Bill O'Hanlon: Thank you for your incredible writing course! Your guidance was invaluable in transitioning this project from a mere collection of thoughts and ideas into an actual book.

To all of my brave clients: Thank you for sharing your stories with me! I am humbled and honored and constantly inspired by you all.

To Heidi Weakley: Thank you for being my first reader and editor (in addition to being part of my beloved T-Town Crew)! Your support and encouragement have ensured that this book actually made it from my laptop into the hands of a publisher.

To my beloved T-Town Crew: Thank you for being my family of choice! You are some of my favorite people on the planet, and I could not think of a more fabulous collection of humans to do life with. Our shared memories are some of my absolute favorites, and I adore each and every one of you.

To Missy: Thank you for your forever brand of friendship! You have been there through it all, and I am so grateful.

To Deb and Sara: Thank you for being my soulmate friends! You both bring me such joy, and our shared laughter over the years has been pure friendship magic.

To Paul: Thank you for being a faithful friend through so many seasons of my life! When I think about the people who have contributed the most to my understanding of meaningful, lasting friendships, you are on the short list.

To all of my friends (from all of the different seasons of my life): Thank you! To my childhood friends in HI, NC, and SC. To my adolescent friends from NMHS, BAG, YL, Northwest University, and Hillcrest. To my adult friends from AGTS, Olive Crest, SRCC, and ECA. To all of my sweet colleagues throughout the years. And to anyone who has done any part of this wild ride with me. You all have provided me with such a rich archive of cherished memories, and I am forever grateful for all of the tender moments and the ridiculous shenanigans.

Thank you for the letters we wrote back and forth throughout our childhood. For our sleepovers. For *all the human videos*. For introducing me to my first caramel mocha (and the Indigo Girls). For our choreographed prom dances. For our late night chats about secret (and not-so-secret) crushes. For my first and last skiing experience. For cruising around in your jalopy listening to ska music. For our week in YL paradise. For our away game shenanigans. For a summer full of pay-per-view movies and steamrolling. For that glorious surprise visit in your 80's prom dresses (with accompanying roller skates). For the secret(ish) DV8 excursions. For all of the late-night Shari's study sessions. For Spring Break 98. For our matching sweater vests (and sweet acapella ditty's). For our Leonardo DiCaprio hunt through Seattle (April Fools). For our friend photo shoots. For our last-minute, frantic, paper writing all-nighters. For the Roomies' adventures. For fish funerals. For the epic car karaoke. For my Christian Bale reeducation. For summer camp dance parties. For extra long lunches. For our "song inspired" car deliveries. For the precarious river tubing escapade. For our "Tour de' South." For bonding retreats. For our pontoon adventure. For all.the.road.trips. For the camping mishaps. For the hideous (but now hilarious) Saint Louis road trip in my ancient VW. For the infamous Coupeville lunch. For Cancun study sessions. For an afternoon of snow-mobiling (fashionable helmets, to boot). For our White Elephant gift exchanges (especially those involving fertility statues). For laser tag birthdays. For that glorious *Sound of Music* sing-along. For NKOTB. For our shared experiences at the Dream Center. For Chatelherault! For our BFF Leavenworth trip. For our Band of Brothers and Domino's pizza bonding nights. For laughing until we cried (and some of us peed our pants). For our evening of salsa dancing. For long distance phone calls. For the red sheets. For our Christmas sing-alongs. For our hot tub Hannah's. For the shock game initiation. For nose bling and friendship bracelet tattoos. For all of the birthdays, graduations, engagements, promotions, weddings, baby showers, and other special celebrations. For *all the friendship things*!

To my family: Thank you for always loving me and supporting me in my endeavors! So much of what I know about being a good friend and human I learned first in my relationships with you all, and I am truly grateful for each of you. Special shoutout to my sweet nieces and nephews, who are the absolute joys of my life!

To the love of my life: Thank you for being the most patient and supportive and steady and generous partner a girl could ask for! You have read and reread this book more times than any human should have to read anything. And you still love it . . . and me. Your unconditional love and tireless cheerleading are the sustenance of my life. And I love you more than all the things.

MY FRIENDSHIP BOOKSHELF

I am including a list of books that make my friendship shortlist, the ones that actually live on my bookshelves. This list includes novels that depict the truest forms of friendship, and also those that remind us that creating and sustaining friendships can be difficult at times. I have included books that can help us increase our friendship-making skills, as well as those that can help us be the best and most available versions of ourselves. Additionally, there are a couple of autobiographies that provide real life stories about the value of friendship, as well as the struggle. I am hopeful that these books will provide you with some supplemental resources for continuing your commitment to meaningful, enduring friendships.

A Man Called Ove by Fredrik Backman
Summer Sisters by Judy Blume
Daring Greatly by Brene Brown
The Five Love Languages by Gary Chapman
Loneliness: Human Nature and the Need for Social Connection by John Cacioppo & William Patrick
Boundaries by Henry Cloud and John Townsend
Beaches by Iris Rainer Dart
The Oxford Book of Friendship by D.J. Enright & David Rawlinson
Inspired by Rachel Held Evans
Fried Green Tomatoes at the Whistle Stop Café by Fannie Flagg
The Relationship Cure by John Gottman
Of Mess and Moxie by Jen Hatmaker
Eleanor Oliphant is Completely Fine by Gail Honeyman
A Thousand Splendid Suns by Khaled Hosseini
Is Everyone Hanging Out Without Me? by Mindy Kaling
Lilac Girls by Martha Hall Kelly
The Dance of Connection by Harriet Lerner
Social: Why Our Brains Are Wired to Connect by Matthew Lieberman
Carry on, Warrior by Glennon Doyle Melton
Love Warrior by Glennon Doyle Melton
Anne of Green Gables (all of them) by L.M. Montgomery
Truth and Beauty by Ann Patchett
Harry Potter (all of them) by J.K. Rowling
The Beautiful No by Sheri Salata
The Norton Book of Friendship by Ronald Sharp & Eudora Welty
The Joy Luck Club by Amy Tan
Lord of the Rings (all of them) by J.R.R. Tolkien
Alone Together by Sherry Turkle
The Color Purple by Alice Walker
Divine Secrets of the Ya-Ya Sisterhood by Rebecca Wjells
Wolfpack by Abby Wambach
The Social Sex by Marilyn Yalom & Theresa Donovan Brown

SUBSCRIBE TO EVERYTHING WE PUBLISH!

Do you love what Microcosm publishes?

Do you want us to publish more great stuff?

Would you like to receive each new title as it's published?

Subscribe as a BFF to our new titles and we'll mail them all to you as they are released!

$13-30/mo, pay what you can afford!

microcosmpublishing.com/bff

...AND HELP US GROW YOUR SMALL WORLD!

More for mastering friendships: